THE PURPLE PAGES

by
Jeffrey Feinman

Hawthorn Books, Inc.
Publishers
New York

A Howard & Wyndam Company

THE PURPLE PAGES

Copyright © 1979 by Ventura Associates, Inc. Copyright under International and PanAmerican Copyright Conventions. All rights reserved, including the right to reproduce this book or portions thereof in any form, except for the inclusion of brief quotations in a review. All inquiries should be addressed to Hawthorn Books, Inc., 260 Madison Avenue, New York, New York 10016. This book was manufactured in the United States of America and published simultaneously in Canada by Prentice-Hall of Canada, Limited, 1870 Birchmount Road, Scarborough, Ontario.

Library of Congress Catalog Card Number: 78-61576

ISBN: 0-8015-6132-9

1 2 3 4 5 6 7 8 9 10

TABLE OF CONTENTS

INTRODUCTION — 1

Chapter 1
KEEPING CLEAR: How to Avoid Problem Situations — 3

Chapter 2
THE A B C's OF COMPLAINING — 15

Chapter 3
CASE HISTORIES — 35

Chapter 4
STATE CONSUMER AGENCIES — 53

Chapter 5
COMPLAINING TO THE MANUFACTURERS — 92

Chapter 6
THE BETTER BUSINESS BUREAU — 115

Chapter 7
FEDERAL AGENCIES — 129

Chapter 8
TRADE ASSOCIATIONS — 151

Chapter 9
SMALL CLAIMS COURT — 156

Chapter 10
MEDIA AND ACTION LINES — 176

Chapter 11
SPECIFIC COMMUNITY HELP — 186

Chapter 12
SPECIFIC PROBLEMS — 196

INTRODUCTION

* The phone company has wrongly disconnected your service.

* Your new toaster burns every slice to a charred crisp.

* You made a reservation in March, but are bumped off your flight to Los Angeles in April.

* Your brand new car won't start on a hill.

* Your landlord refuses to give you heat in December.

The average consumer is faced with thousands of purchase decisions annually and each one of them has, inherent in them, possible disappointments. What's even worse, the new industrial America often leaves the consumer talking to non-responsive computers and non-caring powerless clerks.

"You could turn purple trying to get help," says the average consumer. Fear not, it's THE PURPLE PAGES to the rescue. Here's a detailed compilation of who to call and write to in order to get action for your consumer complaint.

This is not a theoretical book of consumerism. Rather it is an action directory of the names, addresses and phone numbers of those who can help. It guides you through the bureaucratic maze right to the proper agency or person in any given situation.

Although some may find this surprising, most businesses are honest. Surely there are as many dishonest doctors, lawyers, and bricklayers as businessmen. Unfortunately, in business it's often difficult to <u>find</u> the person who wants to help. For example, the president of Woolworth's would probably seek to solve your every complaint; unfortunately you never get to meet him. So, all too often, the entire Woolworth Company takes the form of the sales clerk who is uninterested in your problem.

As a businessman, I know that consumers are the ultimate test of the game. My experience is that this is true for most businesses, even big corporations. Yet in this age of computers often there is sadly no one to speak with. THE PURPLE PAGES is not a consumerist's attack on business, but rather a guide to achieving your goals within the framework of the universe's finest economic system.

Chapter 1: KEEPING CLEAR

The <u>Purple</u> <u>Pages</u> is mainly a directory and advisory guide for people who have something to complain about. Here, you'll find out who to contact and what to say when the refrigerator goes on the blink or the lights go out or the roof starts leaking. But a gram of prevention, as they say, is worth a kilo of cure. So before you go on to the how-to manual for the Complete Complainer, please accept some advice about how to stay out of trouble in the first place.

1. <u>Never</u> <u>buy</u> <u>on</u> <u>impulse</u>. Like all rules, this one has its exceptions, but they are few and far between. Impulse buying is like gambling: you have some chance to win, but the odds are against you. Shun like the plague salespeople who try to get you to sign on the spot, without giving you time to think it over. This can be very hard to do, when you're threatened with the loss of some item you covet. "Three other people were looking at this one about an hour ago," the man in the showroom will say. "We don't have any more like it. This is the last one at this price. Better grab it before someone else does." Don't let yourself be pressured! There is almost nothing so unique that you have to rush into a purchase without considering it until you feel satisfied. Some salespeople, of the slightly unscrupulous variety, will try to make you feel foolish for taking a lot of time over a major purchase. Simply tell them that you haven't made up your mind yet and that if they don't like the way you do business,

you'll be glad to take your money elsewhere. Threatened with the loss of a sale, such people usually let up on the pressure.

2. <u>Consult sources for a best buy</u>. There are lots of periodicals and paperbacks on the market that carry ratings of popular consumer items. Of these, probably the most trustworthy is <u>Consumer Reports</u>, the publication of the Consumer's Union. <u>CR</u> takes no advertising, and is thus not in a position to be swayed by manufacturers who are also sources of revenue for the magazine. In other magazines and books, you can find details of how to select an appliance, a pair of eyeglasses, a home. The better informed you are about the principles that govern excellence in the item you are about to buy, the more likely you are to make a good choice.

Besides general consumer publications, you can consult specialized sources that cover only the item you want to buy. There are any number of magazines, for example, devoted to cameras and photography, and just as many that concentrate on hi-fi equipment or home electronics. In the case of a really large purchase, such as a new house, you can receive a mailbag full of literature and brochures by writing or calling trade associations or contractors (consult your local telephone directory). All the large moving companies distribute pamphlets about how to get your money's worth out of a move. In addition, the U.S. Government Printing Office in Colorado Springs, Colorado, will send you a list of publications, many of them free, on how to buy wisely and save money.

In researching a substantial purchase, don't forget the public library. All of the publications listed above, except possibly some of the government pamphlets, are available for the asking at the library. You may also be able to find full-length books about the industry or type of product that interests you. Ralph Nader and his associates have published several such books, including the famous <u>Unsafe at Any Speed</u>, which deals with the automobile industry. Ask your librarian to suggest other avenues of investigation.

3. <u>Know your merchant</u>. Before you make a significantly large purchase (anything more than a quart of milk these days) be sure the firm you deal with is honest. If you're buying a national brand, chances are the manufacturer stands behind the product, no matter who sells it to you. But discounted merchandise, clothes with the labels out, or off-brands may depend on the seller for warranty and service. If you have any doubts about a company, call your local Better Business Bureau (see Chapter 6, Page 115) and ask if there have been any complaints about this firm. Talk to people you know, particularly if you can find someone who has bought something in the same place. If a merchant has a uniformly bad reputation in the community, it's better to stay away, even if there is no solid information proving shoddy dealing. Whenever possible, buy locally. Merchants in your immediate neighborhood are especially eager to have the goodwill of those close to home. Besides, if your new gizmo should ever need service, repair, or replacement, the whole business will be infinitely easier if you only have to take it down the block.

4. <u>Read the fine print</u>. If there are any warranties or other written commitments from retailer or manufacturer, study them <u>before</u> you plunk your money down. It's an amazing fact that most consumers

don't take the time to find out what's coming to them if anything goes wrong -- even if the purchase is something as major as a car. A large number of customers don't even bother to send back the card that puts their warranty into effect after the purchase is made. When you consider the difference that seller or manufacturer commitments to service can make -- sometimes thousands of dollars -- it seems incredible that so many people don't seem to care.

If your purchase requires you to sign anything -- a lease, a service contract, a contract for time payments -- be sure you really read every bit of it. In the case of very expensive items, have your lawyer go over the contract, too. If you don't have a lawyer, as ninety percent of us don't, you might consider one of the new, low-cost legal clinics that are springing up all across the country. At these clinics, standard legal services are much cheaper than the fifty or sixty dollars an hour charged by private attorneys. If your income is below a certain level, you may be eligible for free legal services through Legal Aid in your community.

5. <u>Pay by check</u>. Using a personal check instead of cash gives you a built-in proof of purchase as well as some control over your money should anything go wrong. If your new mini-bike turns out to be a mini-lemon from the first spin around the block, you can have your bank stop payment on the check. Once your check has cleared the bank, of course, this option is lost to you, but it does give you a few days of home trial time, with a guaranteed refund if you are dissatisfied. If you buy from a store where you have a charge account, you have even longer to test the quality of the product. When the bill comes, simply

refuse to pay the charge for your unsatisfactory purchase. In these, as in all complaint strategies, be sure your gripe is reasonable. If you and the mini-bike have had a run-in with a lamp post, for instance, your complaint that the silly thing won't go amounts to a kind of fraud. In most cases, retailers and manufacturers are very good at spotting the kind of petty cheater who tries to pretend that damage done is some defect of workmanship or design in the product. But if you have used the product according to specifications and not abused it, you have every right to refuse to pay for it. Naturally, you will also return the merchandise as soon as possible.

In the case of time payments or installments, it's never a good idea to just stop paying, unless you have given your creditor notice of your reasons. You could do unnecessary damage to your credit rating that way, and once these black marks have been digested by the credit bureau's computers, they are very hard to extract. Most of us would rather not be involved in time payments and the extra charges they entail, but it's often a good idea to buy this way, even if you have the full price on hand, and then pay the rest off after you take delivery. That way, you have some leverage if delivery is held up, and there will be less money to try to get back if you have to cancel your order.

6. <u>Play by the rules</u>. If your warranty says that the vacuum cleaner should be washed once a year with soap and lemon juice, do it, no matter how silly you think it is. Read all the instructions that come with any new product, even if you've been operating one for forty years and think you know all about it. Or, if you insist on playing

fast and loose with this carefully designed little piece of engineering wizardry, don't be offended when it starts spraying sparks and won't cut hair any more. Remember, if you have not complied in every way with the operating instructions supplied to you, chances are you won't get a refund, even if the defect really is in the works. A consumer from Iowa recently had to pay for the repair of an obviously faulty electrical system in his new foreign car, just because he had replaced the foreign-made spark plugs with an American brand, contrary to the service manual's instructions.

7. <u>Take the time to listen</u>. You are much less likely to be disappointed in a product if you really understand everything it can and cannot do for you. Make sure you ask the salesperson every last question that crosses your mind, and don't let him hurry over the answers. When ordering by mail, it's a good idea to spell out on the order form just what your impression of the product is and why you want it. If you have the wrong idea, you'll probably get an explanation by return mail instead of a thingamajig you can't use. When renting an apartment, ask about everything, even the things that seem "obvious" to you. Nothing is ever really obvious until it's been explicitly stated. Who pays for extermination, if necessary? Who pays for the water? Is garbage collection provided? Especially when you're moving into a strange locality, the answers to such "obvious" questions might surprise you.

A woman in Maryland bought an expensive piece of sterling silver at an exclusive suburban store and took it downstairs to the engraving department to have her daughter's initials put on it. She was shocked when the store billed her thirty dollars for the engraving. Although she had not shopped in the store for many years, she assumed that customers could still get complimentary engraving on substantial purchases. Complain as she might, the fault was on her side for not getting the facts straight before she bought. Never be embarrassed or shy about asking what goods or services cost, including medical or dental services. The doctor, after all, isn't shy about billing you.

8. <u>Be a paper collector</u>. The smart consumer keeps a file of sales slips, operating instructions, copies of letters, contracts, anything and everything in writing that pertains to the products and services he or she buys. Most of the time, such things just become keepsakes, memorabilia with no further use. But once in a while, that file full of old papers can save you a bundle of paper of a more valuable sort. A mother of four in Tennessee says she saves all the tags from her children's clothes if they mention a period during which the garment is supposed to remain serviceable. "Most of the time," she reports with surprise, "the shirt or whatever it is wears out before the time is up. I'd say more often than not. You'd think they wouldn't keep guaranteeing these things, but they do." By returning the clothes that don't stand her family's test of time, this woman manages to stretch her clothes budget half again as far as she could otherwise. Now she always looks for such guarantees and always keeps track of how long the clothes really last. For a manufacturer, promises of this sort have strong selling power. Even if the company is forced to make good on the promise to a few consumers, many more will forget the guarantee, and simply shrug it off if the garment wears out early. Retailers and manufacturers count on consumer indifference to

keep the costs of their promises low, but they are usually quite willing to stand by their words, if anybody has bothered to remember what they were.

9. <u>Know your rights</u>. When something does go wrong, is it really the kind of thing you're entitled to get mad about? Some people get angry too quickly, others not quickly enough. Did you know, for instance, that you cannot be held to the terms of a contract you've signed if the contract is illegal? Did you know that some warranty is implied with every product, even if no written material is given to you? Nobody is allowed to sell you a house unfit for habitation, for example, and then say, "Well, who ever told you you could live in it? Did I say that?" Just by selling you a house, a vendor implies that it will perform, at least minimally, the normal functions of a house. If the advertising of a product says that it will clear up your acne -- and you can prove that the product has no effect on acne -- you are entitled to a refund, even if the package contains no <u>guarantee</u> per se. In a recent decision, a well-known singing star and his daughter were ordered to stop saying that a skin product worked. They paid back -- out of their own pockets -- some of the money ordered refunded to customers.

Most people who start to educate themselves about the ins and outs of modern consumerism get hooked. They become consumer information buffs to one degree or another, eager to read the next independent testing lab survey of pocket toasters, even if they never intend to toast a pocket in their lives. The more you know about consumerism in general, the less chance that you'll get taken in any specific market interaction. You don't have to be a lawyer to find such information, either. Most consumer agencies and Better Business Bureaus can get you started with a mailbox full of free pamphlets. Media "action lines" are especially good for filling you in on just what you are and aren't entitled to in a specific situation. Newspapers have legal experts whose job it is to be up on all the current legislation and its applications to individual problems. In every case, don't hesitate to ask.

10. <u>Understand the specifics of each case</u>. If you are buying from a department store, know that store's policy with respect to returns, credits, refunds: do they make it easy for you to exchange merchandise, or is it hard? When dealing with a utility or the phone company, be sure you watch the bills for unreasonable charges. This sort of thing can slip by unnoticed, especially if you live in an area where the phone company charges for message units even within the local calling area. Be sure a friend or family member isn't responsible for abnormally high bills.

When renting or buying a place in which to live, one of the most important aspects is the character of the seller or landlord. If he or she is a person of good will, someone you feel you can trust to be considerate of you in the really important matters, this counts more than contractual responsibility. Yes, your landlord is required to make the place livably warm in the winter, and yes, you can take him to court and win if he doesn't. But court proceedings take a long time, and you might be freezing all that while. If you do get stuck with a landlord who only wants to collect the rent and refuses to provide minimal services, move out. Should the landlord give you any trouble about breaking your lease, you can give him a lot more trouble right back from the housing authority, department of health, your elected representatives and your lawyer. Many consumer publications offer a lot of advice about how to force your landlord to make repairs, give heat, and so on. But unless you are willing to devote months and years to a rent strike or other legal battle, you are better off looking for a new place to live. If you are the sort who has time and energy for a tenant's organization, such groups can and have accomplished wonders in upgrading buildings and neighborhoods. You can get organizational help from consumer groups and sympathetic public officials.

When it comes to medical matters, most consumers are dreadfully ignorant of what constitutes good service. Incompetent doctors and dentists -- of whom there are a few -- depend on this ignorance and on the tendency of sick people to have a child-like and sometimes unjustified faith in the person they hope will make everything better. Try to be alert to negligence or poor treatment, even when you are ill. If you have any doubts about the quality of medical or dental treatment you are given, insist on the opinion of an outside consultant. When buying prescription drugs, ask the doctor to write the generic name of the drug instead of the brand name, and be sure the druggist gives you the amount specified in the proper strength. In states where advertising of drug prices and fees for eyeglasses are allowed, there are great differences among different establishments. Take advantage of discounts and lower prices as long as you are sure the services are the same.

If you are travelling or moving, precautions prior to the trip can save you months or even years of headaches later. When you travel, even if you go in your own car, put labels on everything. Don't put up with overbooking, either at hotels or on public transportation. Airlines are required to either put you on another flight within two hours or give your money back while letting you keep your ticket. (The ticket can later be exchanged or you can get another refund.) On foreign flights, the time limit is four hours. Airlines must also find you a place to stay until you can continue your trip, and they have to pay for it. This applies only to U.S. companies, however, and only if you show up for your reserved flight on time.

More people experience pain, loss, and distress over moving than just about any other consumer activity. Moving is upsetting enough, even when everything goes well. And once the plans you've made for getting your things across town or across the country go haywire, the result can be chaos. Fortunately, there's a lot of help available from the moving companies, industry associations, and public bodies. The single thing that can make all the difference between a good and a bad move is planning. The longer in advance you start to map your move, the better it will go. Leave yourself plenty of time to get estimates, talk to friends about their experiences, and coordinate all the dates and times. Make lists of all the questions you want to ask the moving companies, so you won't forget. Most people move during the spring and summer, and there are good reasons for it, as you probably know. But if you possibly can, move during the off season (October-April). Part of what makes for all those foul-ups in moving is the crushing demand during the warm months.

When buying a new car, or a new-to-you car, be sure you research the purchase thoroughly in advance. A car is one of the biggest expenses most families have, but it need not be one of the biggest headaches if you take your time about it. In the case of a new car, be sure of what you want before you ever enter a dealer's showroom. Once there, be persistent until you get satisfactory answers to <u>all</u> your questions. Don't let yourself be talked into a more expensive car than you want and need, and don't let the salesman gloss over such important matters as warranty, trade-in allowance, and available options. A certain kind of sharpie will lead you right up to the moment of decision before he reveals that he doesn't quite have what you want, in the color you want, but he can give you the same car in yellow, if you don't mind paying a tiny bit extra for a tape deck and white sidewalls. When this happens, it's your cue to walk off the lot.

In the case of a used car, the most important action you can take is to have the car checked over by an independent mechanic. If the seller won't allow this, forget the deal. The chief disadvantage to buying a used car is not that it has been driven before, but that you have no way of knowing <u>how</u> it has been driven. If you buy from a dealer, there will usually be a short-term (60-90 day) warranty. Be sure you understand the terms of the warranty, and that you get the car right back to the dealer if anything goes wrong. Used-car dealers are notorious for operating on the shady side of the truth, so check yours out with the Better Business Bureau before you buy.

Chapter 2:
THE A B C's OF COMPLAINING

If there is a single outstanding principle of consumer complaining, it is that you have to know what you want before you start. Successful fighters-back in the marketplace have had just about as many different specific strategies as there are things to complain about. But the one thing they all have in common is a determination to reach a specific goal by complaining. Once in a while, the goal is simply to chastise a clerk or executive who has been uncooperative or shifty. More often, the goal is compensation for whatever trouble the consumer has suffered. Successful complainers never want just to be heard, to vent their anger, or to be given vague reassurances. They want <u>action</u>. They want something in particular -- settled on <u>before</u> they are purple with rage -- that will repair or cancel out the damage that has been done.

Once you have decided exactly, in minute detail, what you want to win by complaining, the specific steps you should take will be self-evident. Not knowing where to start with a complaint is often a symptom of not knowing what your goal is, or of not making it sufficiently clear and concrete in your mind. The very first thing you should do when you run into an error in your phone bill or a shirt that disintegrates in the wash or a new car that makes a grinding noise when you start it or a new house that doesn't have all the features you were promised -- in short, when you run into any problem of any size -- is sit down and decide just exactly what state of affairs would constitute a solution to the problem. You may be willing to settle for the disappearance of the grinding noise, for instance, or you may be so nervous about the possibility of failure on the road that you also want a written assurance from the manufacturer that the noise doesn't represent a dangerous structural defect. If you haven't paid the incorrect bill, you probably just want the extra charges deleted. But, if you have already taken your money out of the bank to pay for false charges, you might also want the phone company to pay you interest on the funds they have been "borrowing" from you. Whatever your goal in complaining might be, it is absolutely essential to spell it out to yourself at the beginning. In this, as in all matters of consumer protection, you should put what you want <u>in writing</u>. That way, there can be no confusion later on, when things have begun to get thick.

Now suppose you have given the matter some thought and have written on your battle chart that you won't be satisfied until you get a new pair of shoes, similar in style and fit to the old ones, but better-made, so that they don't come unglued after a week. How to proceed? There are no unbreakable rules about this, of course, and many of the most successful consumer complainers are those with somewhat offbeat styles. Normally, however, the steps will be something like these:

<u>First</u>, collect all the data you might have that pertains to the problem. Shrewd consumers save receipts, warrantees, and care instructions, at least for a few months after a purchase. The bigger

the price tag, the longer such things should be saved. In the case of something really big, like a house or a car, papers should be permanently filed. If there are no papers, as in the case of fraudulent statements made by a salesman in person, write down everything you can recall about the transaction: time, day, exact words, everything.

Second, decide <u>to whom you will complain</u>. In every case, it helps to have names. Whether you have to get in touch with an undersecretary of state or the lady who works at the flower shop during the lunch hour, you'll do it more quickly if you know their names. If you don't know any names, make a preliminary inquiry before you start to complain. Certain companies -- big credit-card outfits, for example -- have a way of giving you code names that don't belong to any real people, such direction actually identifies you as someone with a bug in her ear. This won't happen if you get the names you want before you let anybody know you have a gripe. Otherwise, you may be in the frustrating position of being put on "hold" for an hour, or having your letter sent to the corporate equivalent of the dead letter office.

<u>Third</u>, choose your first approach. Often, but not always, this will be the telephone. Your specific problem will determine how you begin. If you have a piece of defective merchandise to return to a department store, it is almost surely a waste of time to call the store. If the item is small enough, you should take it right back to the department in which it was purchased and preferably to the very person who sold it to you. (It might be worth while calling the store and asking for your salesperson, if you know his or her name. You can

at least find out what hours that person will be available.) If the item is large, something like a freezer or a piece of furniture, you should go to the store and talk to the salesperson to arrange for the store to either fix or take away the offending item. In many other cases, using the phone will save you considerable frustration. There's no use taking your new car in to the dealer to have that "ping" fixed, only to be told that they'd be glad to do it, but the mechanic won't be back until Wednesday. You could have found that out on the phone. In still other cases, the telephone is the method of choice. Lots of busy executives, who wouldn't think of seeing you if you showed up in their reception rooms, will answer the phone without hesitation.

Once you decide that the telephone should be your first line of attack, take a deep breath and resolve not to get angry, at least not so that it shows. Sarcasm, hysteria, shouting, obscenity, and outlandish threats will only get you labelled as a nut. The most effective style is calm, cool, measured -- even while you are saying rather aggressive things. If you keep an even tone, you'll be much more likely to be treated with seriousness and respect. Unless you have some reason to believe it won't work, you'll probably want to start by calling the specific division set up by the seller to handle complaints. In larger stores and corporations, this is usually called something like "customer service." When you call, come right to the point. Describe your problem in condensed detail, and then describe exactly what you want the seller to do for you. Sometimes, if your complaint and your request are simple and clear, the difficulty will end right there. "Of course we'll send you out the missing part," the complaints person will say. "You'll probably get it in Friday's mail."

More often than not, however, you will be referred, kept waiting, and referred again. You will be told to call back in two hours, a day, a week. Always keep a record of these calls; be sure to take down the names of the people you talk to, the date and time of the calls, and the promises made. As your case progresses, you will be able to say, "Look, on March 29, Miss Addison in the customer relations department told me that part would arrive the next Friday. It is now April 12. I think, to compensate me for the additional delay, you should send out a repairman with the part, and have him put the dishwasher together." (It's a good idea to escalate your demands if you feel you're being given the run-around. If the stakes seem to be going up, the management may become more eager to settle with you.)

If you are not successful in your use of the telephone within a reasonable time, the next step will very likely be a letter of complaint. For some reason, a single letter often gets prompt results, even where several phone calls have failed. Whether this is because people have more respect for the written than the spoken word, or because they are more inclined to respond to someone who has taken the time to put it down in black and white, it is a fact that more positive results are obtained through letters than through any other method. Since this is the case, a great deal of attention has already been devoted to showing people how to write a good letter of complaint. Several consumer publications have printed articles about the best way to compose such a letter.

Perhaps the best way to develop a knack for the effective letter is to develop your own forms. Once you have composed a few winning letters of complaint, you'll have a little arsenal of model letters to use in the future. Don't forget to make and keep copies of all consumer correspondence, even if you don't think it's prize-winning prose. You may need the evidence for the next round. Some sample letters are given below, but first; the general principles:

<u>Appearance</u>: Looks aren't everything, but they aren't nothing, either. There are very few cases in which it is better to send a crumpled, grubby, handwritten note than a neatly typed business letter on good stationery. (The exceptional cases are: 1. You are under ten years old. 2. You simply want to avoid having anything more to do with the recipient of the letter. If you are being harassed for payments on a set of encyclopedias you never bought, paid for, or laid eyes on, the "insane letter" may work as a last resort. If they think you are utterly incompetent, they may just write you off as uncollectable.) Unless you are a child or <u>in extremis</u>, stick to the standard business letter, and always type. If you have access to some impressive stationery, say, the letterhead of the school board you serve on, or just something heavy and plain with your name on it, by all means use it. If not, get some good white paper (not eraseable) and begin.

<u>Content</u>: What you say in a complaint letter counts more, of course, than whether or not your typing is perfect. Again, strive to appear businesslike. Certain words and phrases, while they make English teachers blanch and don't really mean much, are signals to the

business community that they are dealing with someone who knows what he or she is doing. "Dear Sir," for example, is still good if you have been unable to obtain a name. If you dislike the assumption that all persons in power are men (which might also put off "dear sir" if she happens to be a woman), use a phrase like, "To the Manager," or leave off the salutation altogether. Don't use "Dear Sir or Madame," or "To Whom It May Concern." These types of letters just don't get attention.

Start all complaint letters the same way you started the complaint process itself: state your aim. Your request should be the very first thing that meets the eye of Ms. or Mr. Manager, before you go into any details about what you bought, when, and why you don't like it. Not only does this instantly make clear to the reader why he or she is being addressed, but it helps you to keep your aim firmly in mind throughout the rest of the letter. Most of all, it gives Ms. Big a reason to go on reading. Why, after all, should she want to read a long story about a refrigerator, even though she works for an appliance company? But if she has already been told that here is a customer demanding a refund or a new refrigerator, she is much more likely to want to find out why.

After you've said what you want, give, as briefly as possible, the history of the transaction. If this is your first letter, this section (try to keep it to a single paragraph) will give as many specifics as you have about what you bought (model numbers and other identifiers), from whom (again, a name is a plus), and when. If you have written before or had other communication about this matter, include that information, too.

Third, state the reason for your complaint. Notice that this isn't the first or even the second thing you do. The most common error made in writing complaint letters is to start immediately with a long tale of woe or rage. No matter how dramatic the details of your suffering, this is almost never the way to go, unless you want to be treated like a nut. To get businesslike results, you must proceed in a businesslike way. Once you have captured your reader's attention with a request and earned his or her respect with your careful documentation, <u>then</u> you can tell how the blasted thing blew dirt all over the living room. It's hard to keep this part brief, especially if you have a long history of trouble. But remember, the object of your complaint isn't to be heard, it's to win. You stand a better chance of getting what you want if you don't bore your reader or try his or her patience.

After the facts have been laid out, with all the details and documentation you can muster, end your letter with a restatement of your request and, very gently at first, the <u>Implied</u> <u>Threat</u>. At the beginning, the best I.T. is just "or else." You might say, for example, "I expect this matter to be settled in two weeks or less." This is much better than the vague, though more polite, "I hope you will take action on this matter quickly." For a first letter, the Implied Threat is enough. If you don't get what you want before the expiration of the deadline, you'll want to use a more explicit threat in subsequent letters, something like: "If this part is not replaced before the end of the month, I will be shipping the air conditioner back to the store, C.O.D." Whatever your threat, be sure it's something you're actually willing to carry out if your requests and demands are not met.

To whom should calls and letters of complaint be addressed? At first, of course, the best line of attack is to stay as close as possible to the actual point of sale. Perhaps your first protest over defective merchandise will be made to the salesperson who helped you. When that doesn't work, you'll move on to the store's complaint department, then the manager, and then perhaps the president of the company. If the retail avenue seems unproductive, don't give up. You have really just begun. The next place to send your well-wrought letters is the manufacturer of the item, if the defect could in any way be attributed to them. If that doesn't work, move on to the Better Business Bureau and the relevant trade associations. When these avenues are exhausted, get in touch with a <u>state</u> or <u>local</u> (in heavily populated areas) <u>consumer protection agency</u>. If such an agency can't help you directly, they can usually advise you whether to seek help from a <u>federal agency</u>, a <u>specialized consumer group</u>, or perhaps from one of the "<u>action lines</u>" maintained by newspapers and other media. The general principle here is to start with the smaller, more localized organizations, and move up to the larger ones if you need to. If you start with the state attorney general's office, you may just be referred back to a smaller group in your area. But if you can say, "Yes, I tried them, they can't help me," the state agency might take more interest in your case.

Finally, there is always room for the unorthodox. Just when

you should decide to stop going through channels and hit the streets with your sandwich board is an individual matter. Many consumers have had good results with picketing, boycotts, midnight phone calls, and newspaper ads. If you ever do decide to use such tactics, beware of saying (or more precisely, writing) something libelous. If you picket a store with a sign that says, "Ace shoes don't fit," you may be guilty of libel. But, if your sign reads, "Ace sold me a pair of shoes that aren't my size and they won't take them back" -- the simple facts of your own case -- you are not committing libel. As Ace probably knows, the effect of you and your sign will be much the same either way -- it will discourage business. The difference is that in the first instance, Ace could sue you, and win. It's a good idea to consult a lawyer before launching a one-person crusade against a manufacturer or retailer who has done you wrong. Often, he or she will suggest that you join a volunteer consumer group and enlist the other members in your struggle. Most activist tactics are more effective when they are group efforts, anyway.

SAMPLE LETTERS

Now that you have collected your throughts and all your receipts, guarantees, and other evidence, you're ready to write. To help you, here are a few good, and not-so-good samples of complaint letters. To begin, here is a hypothetical example of what <u>not</u> to write:

> Dear Gumbles Department Store,
>
> The coffee grinder you sold me doesn't work. Every time I put the beans in the hopper the

way the instructions say, they just pop out again and spray all over the kitchen. One of them hit my husband in the eye the other morning at breakfast, and he says we ought to sue you. I think so too, and we will, if we don't get a new coffee grinder, or at least our money back.

                      Sincerely yours,

                      Dale Wilson

What, exactly, is wrong with this? First, it isn't written in the form of a business letter. You may feel that this kind of thing is just a technicality, and it is. But it's a detail, like shaking hands -- it only matters when you don't do it. Whoever receives this letter -- and that would be anybody's guess, since there is no specific addressee -- will tend to treat it as a trivial matter because the case is not presented formally, according to the customs of business. When in Rome, as they say, speak Italian. And when writing to Gumbles, speak business.

Our bad example does have one virtue -- it's short. This may ensure that it will be read, even though it launches immediately into what went wrong, without the "grabber" of a request first. But the fact that somebody at Gumbles may read the letter won't do Ms. Wilson much good, because she doesn't say specifically enough what she wants. Nor does she give her address or phone number, except possibly on the back of the envelope, in case anyone from the store did want to reach her. It isn't enough just to say, "I want a new coffee grinder." A good complaint letter spells out exactly what the recipient must do to satisfy the dissatisfied consumer. Has Dale tried returning the appliance to the store? If so, why wouldn't they take the return? If not, why not? Does she expect Gumbles to come to her door with a new coffee grinder? Does she want them to mail her one? Since all of these questions are unanswered, and since the letter contains no statement of what the customer will do if her demands are not met, beyond a rather wild threat to "sue," her letter will probably end up in the receptionist's wastebasket. Ms. Wilson would have much better luck with a letter like this:

>   Address
>   City, State, Zip Code
>   Date
>
> Complaint Department
> Gumbles Department Store
> Address
> City, State, Zip Code
>
> To the Complaint Department:
>
>   I am writing to request that your store either replace my Brew Magic Coffee Grinder or refund the $19.95 that I paid for it.
>
>   I purchased the coffee grinder by check from the Housewares Department of Gumbles Downtown store on August 29th of this year. The grinder (Model BM 246-x) comes with a full one-year warranty, which is in effect for another nine months. I enclose photocopies of my check, the sales slip from the transaction, and the warranty.
>
>   In October, the grinder began working badly, would not grind coffee beans, and threw them around the room instead. I called the Housewares Department and was told that if I brought the appliance in, someone would fix it. On October 3rd, I took the coffee grinder down to the store, where a Ms. Efrin in the Housewares Department told me that I would have to take it to Mr. Tolman, in the basement. I did so, and was told by Mr. Tolman that he did not do such jobs, and that somebody had made a mistake. I went home and called the store again, but Ms. Efrin was not available, and the man I talked to would not give his name, saying only

that I should send the grinder back to the manufacturer.

    I feel that since Gumbles advertises that it stands behind every product it sells, you have an obligation to provide me with the coffee grinder I paid for, or return my money. I shall expect to hear within three weeks which you will do.

                      Sincerely,

                        Dale Wilson

Phone number: (507) 334-8767

    A common problem faced by most consumers at one time or another is the faulty bill. If the company is a large one, you can sometimes get such things cleared up very quickly simply by telephoning your assigned "customer representative." Sometimes, however, things are hopelessly gummed up down at C Corporation, and telephone calls only get you another recitation of the same stale (and incorrect) records. The time has come to write. If you have already spoken to the complaint department, shoot for somebody higher up, say, a vice president, and try to sound like a busy and important person yourself (because, of course, you are).

                        Address
                        City, State, Zip Code
                        Date

Mr. John Franklin, Vice President
Department of Public Relations
Big C Credit Company
Address
City, State, Zip Code

Dear Mr. Franklin:

    I would like your company to remove the overcharge and all accumulated interest from my bill before the end of this month.

> For three months, my account (#22-456-9878) has carried a charge in the amount of $450.00, which Mr. William Malm in your Customer Relations office informs me is for ten days' stay at the Miami Sheraton Motor Inn in Miami Beach. Since I have never in my life been further south than Maryland, I am naturally disinclined to pay this bill.
>
> I have spoken with Mr. Malm on three separate dates, April 17, 22, and 23. Each time, he told me that he had searched the records, finding no record of my signature on a bill from the Miami Sheraton, but that the charge cannot be removed until he discovers how it got there, and who really owes the $450.00. In the meantime, I cannot use the credit card, because of outstanding debts.
>
> There is no good reason, as I see it, for your organization to harass and inconvenience me because of a company error. If the erroneous charge is not removed from my bill before the next billing date, I will cancel my account, and make every effort to see that others in my company do the same. Those of us who must travel on business can hardly afford to use a credit card company whose bookkeeping is unreliable.
>
> Sincerely yours,
>
> Morgan W. Morgan

The first good point about this letter is that it is addressed to a specific person with a specific title, showing that the writer has taken the trouble to find out who handles problems of this kind. Almost any business letter will work better for you if it goes to a real individual, and spells his or her name right. Try to get the exact job title, too. People don't like to be addressed as "assistants" when they've been promoted to "chiefs."

In the body of the letter, Mr. Morgan begins with a clear, short statement of his aim. The reader knows from the outset why Mr.

Morgan is writing to him, and what action he expects the company to take. What follows is an explanation of why they should do so. You'll notice that all the important details of the transaction in question and the conversations Mr. Morgan has already had with the company are included. He names names, quotes dates, and includes the exact amount and his account number. The more details of this kind you can insert into a complaint letter, the easier it is for the organization to which you're complaining to check it out.

Last, but not least, Mr. Morgan states what action he will take if his request from the first paragraph of the letter is not met. This is a clear and specific threat to end his dealings with the company, and also to tell associates not to deal with this firm. No business wants customers to take this kind of action, and most will go to all reasonable lengths to prevent incurring a consumer's ill will.

Often, the matter for complaint is not the failure of any product, but the fact that merchandise has never been delivered in the first place. If this is your problem, your letter of complaint might read something like this:

                                      Address
                                      City, State, Zip Code
                                      Date

Customer Relations Division
Sleepy Time Bedding
Address
City, State, Zip Code

Dear Sir:

    This is to inform you that I will not accept delivery on the Kiddy-Snooze Bunk Beds I ordered from your store if they do not arrive by December 1, 1978.

> The bunk beds were purchased on my charge account (#559765-H) on August 23. I was told by the salesperson, Mr. Harry Little, that the beds would have to come from the warehouse, and would be delivered during the last week in September. I arranged for someone to be at home every day that week, but nothing was delivered. Since then, I have called the store, including two phone calls to Mr. Sneeden and Ms. Rusk in your department, but cannot obtain a firm date for delivery of my beds. I hardly know who to address my letter to, since neither of these people has been very helpful.
>
> Enclosed please find copies of my sales slip, with the notation of a September delivery date. I can be reached at my office for notification of delivery time, but must have a week's notice in order to arrange for someone to receive the beds. If I don't hear from you before November 24, please cancel my order and my charge account.
>
> Sincerely,
>
> Betty Buyer
>
> Office Phone: (415) 533-8790

Note the importance of taking the time to get the exact name of the department to which you are writing. You may not think there's much difference between Customer Relations and Customer Service, for instance, but it makes a big difference to the people who work there. It is as annoying to them (and counterproductive to you) to get the name of their department or division wrong as it is to hear their personal names mispronounced.

For some consumer problems, there is no real remedy. If a company employee has been rude to you, there is no way the firm can undo the damage. You can, however, obtain an apology, and you can prevent the same thing happening a second time, to you or to someone else. It is especially important in such cases to address your complaint to somebody in middle or upper management, somebody who is likely to care about the company image and the loss of public good will.

                                      Address
                                      City, State, Zip Code
                                      Date

Ms. Jennifer Logan, Manager
Customer Services
Tri-City Rapid Transit Company
Address
City, State, Zip Code

Dear Ms. Logan:

    I would like an apology from your company for the treatment my daughter and I received from one of your drivers last week.

    Every Wednesday I take my daughter, who is eight, downtown to her swimming lesson. For the last few weeks, we have been taking the bus because I feel we should all use public transportation more, and that we should teach our children to conserve energy.

    Last Wednesday, however, my daughter got a lesson in why <u>not</u> to take the bus. To begin with, your driver, Mr. Black, closed the door in front of us, even though we had been waiting in line with the other passengers. When I complained, he said he didn't realize we were waiting for his bus. Since there was no other bus scheduled to stop at that corner, it's hard to understand how he made the mistake. After he did let us on, your Mr. Black ignored my questions about the new stops added to the bus route, and argued with my daughter about her student's pass, even though she is quite obviously not old enough to be anything but a student. Finally, he passed our stop completely, letting us off in a rather dangerous place in the middle of the block instead of at the corner.

    I hope you will find out what is troubling Mr. Black (he wouldn't tell me his first name) and that such incidents will happen less often on our city busses. It will be instructive

> for both me and my daughter to see whether we receive an apology for this really shabby treatment of paying customers.
>
> Sincerely,
>
> Sandy Brown

There will naturally be times when even the most persuasively written letter will fall short of your goals. You still haven't seen hide nor hair of those bunkbeds, and the deadline is only a week away. You can carry out your threat to cancel, of course, but you're still left with the problem of where the twins are going to sleep. That's why you went out and spent your hard-earned money on bunkbeds in the first place. You may want to give the store another chance, in the form of a second letter of complaint. And if your problem is one which has left you holding the bag -- or the malfunctioning merchandise -- you will surely want to write one or more follow-up letters. When you do, don't forget to include carbons or photocopies of all previous letters, and make a notation at the bottom about where you are sending any additional copies: to the Better Business Bureau, for example, to your lawyer, or to a government agency. Always keep at least one copy of every complaint letter for your own files.

Once you begin to stand up for your rights as a consumer, you'll find that subsequent problems are easier to handle. Many people are fearful of complaining, afraid that they will be somehow punished for starting something unpleasant, even when they are sure they have been injured. If your complaints follow good form and are never abusive, libelous, or gratuitously insulting, you can usually expect a polite response, if not a genuine solution on the first round. You may discover that consumer assertiveness (not aggressiveness) makes all your dealings in the marketplace more competent and rewarding.

And speaking of rewards, what about those occasions when something outstandingly good has happened to you in your role as a consumer of goods and services? Don't those who go out of their way to please and help us deserve praise every bit as much as those who don't deserve complaints? Most people -- even accomplished complainers -- forget this aspect of the consumer responsibility. As long as everything is going well, they offer no comment. But often a single letter of praise will do more to raise the morale and the service of a firm than twenty tiresome complaints to be answered. Consumer praise is not only a matter of justice, but also of mercy. You may be smoothing the path for yourself and for every other customer of the establishment you praise. Just once in a while, if you're lucky enough to experience some really outstanding pleasantry, take the time to send a letter of praise:

>   Address
>   City, State, Zip Code
>   Date
>
> Mr. Arthur Dodge, President
> Candy Co., Inc.
> Address
> City, State, Zip Code
>
> Dear Mr. Dodge:
>
>   I am writing to commend you on the thoughtul service we have received from your company.
>
>   Last week, I bought a box of your chocolate creams for my mother. When she opened the box, it was evident that the candy was very old, much beyond the age after which it should have been removed from the shelf. I took the

candy back to Marshall's Candy Store, where I bought it, and they gave me a fresh box, which my mother enjoyed.

On Monday morning, an employee of your firm called me to say that he was sorry we had had a bad experience with Candy Co. candy, and he offered to send me a new box. When I told him we had already exchanged the candy for a satisfactory box, he said the company would like me to have a new box anyway, with his compliments.

I am truly grateful for companies like yours that take the time to put right mistakes made in their names, and for the courtesy of your employee, Mr. Hugo Barton. You can be sure that, as a result of this experience, you have at least one family of absolutely loyal customers.

                          Sincerely,

                          Betty Buyer

Chapter 3:
CASE HISTORIES

The better prepared you are to complain, the more likely you are to get action on your complaint. And there's nothing like knowing how other consumers have wrung satisfaction out of the system to get you ready for the day you have to take pen or telephone or bullhorn in hand yourself. There are almost as many ways to proceed with a consumer complaint as there are chipped cups, fuzzy picture tubes or wrongly-sized blouses to complain about. Some complainers do best with letters, others need face-to-face contact to be fully effective. Still others -- a small but noticeable minority -- have the best luck with unorthodox ploys such as picketing or the midnight call to an executive's bedside. It's a matter of fitting the technique to the situation and to your personality.

If you have always been the timid type who would rather just throw out the defective alarm clock than make a scene, don't worry. You don't have to make a scene to get fair treatment. Marcia Zarelli feels the same way, yet she's one of the most successful complainers in her town. People who don't know her very well assume that Marcia must have to go through a lot of shouting matches to win as many consumer battles as she has. Nothing could be further from the truth. Last year, for example, Marcia was faced with a situation that could have cost her hundreds of dollars. Her car registration had come due, and she had mailed the check to her state's motor vehicles department in plenty of time. But somehow something went wrong down at the old bureaucracy. The deadline came and went, and Marcia received no new registration stickers to put on her car. She began to receive tickets for expired registration, which, of course, she didn't pay. Soon, the tickets collected penalties, and Marcia was well on her way to a gigantic tab with the state.

After two or three letters to the department of motor vehicles brought no response, Marcia decided she had to face an in-person visit to the Capitol. As she well knew, the lines at the registration department would be impossible -- dozens of hot, weary, angry car owners, missing work, standing in line for hours, getting the frustrating run-around when their turn finally did come. As she took her place behind all the other grim-faced taxpayers, Marcia sized up the situation. This was certainly a miserable scene for the people, like herself, who simply had to get some matter straightened out. And, she reflected, it was a pretty miserable scene for the clerks behind those windows, too. As person after person finally made it to the head of the line, little explosions would take place. Tempers flared, voices were raised, fists were shaken. Once, Marcia saw a clerk call a burly male supervisor to escort a shouting man from the room.

Marcia made up her mind that no matter how long she had to wait, she would not lose her temper. After all, what she wanted was satisfaction, a way out of her difficulty, not revenge. As the minutes dragged by and her ankles began to hurt, she reminded herself that those people who let their irritations show were also losing their chance to talk to somebody who could -- if they wanted to --

solve the problem. "I said to myself," Marcia recalls, "How can I make that clerk <u>want</u> to help me?"

Then, the wait was over at last, and Marcia was actually face-to-face with a human representative of the state. She had her cancelled check and all her police citations in her hand, but she did not slap them down on the counter. Instead, she gave the harried clerk a friendly smile and said, "This sure is one heck of a busy day for you, isn't it?"

The effect was electric. The clerk looked at Marcia as though she were the first human being he had seen in months. "It sure is," he said gratefully, wiping his forehead. "Everybody's in a big hurry, and everybody's mad."

Marcia smiled an even bigger smile. She told him she knew just how it was, that she worked in the same kind of place, and it was really hard to help everybody out, especially when you were always under pressure. (In fact, Marcia sells real estate and is almost never in the office for more than twenty minutes, but it was the kind of white lie that helps smooth everyone's path in situations like this.)

"Well," said the clerk, "maybe you'll be the one I <u>can</u> do something for today. What brings you here?" So Marcia explained, sweetly and slowly, all about her expired registration and the tickets. The clerk said that sort of information wasn't kept on file in the office, but he'd be glad to run upstairs and get her file, if she could wait. She could. Within minutes, he returned with the name of someone on the third floor who would handle her problems for her, find the error, and take care of the citations, too, so she wouldn't have to waste time in court. "Joe's a friend of mine," smiled the clerk, "and he's in his office now. I told him I'd send you right up."

Half an hour later, Marcia had a special temporary sticker for her car. Four days after that, she received a permanent sticker in the mail, along with notification that her fines had been cancelled. "You know," she says, "that man didn't have to go upstairs and find help for me. It wasn't part of his job, and it probably saved me a lot of time and grief. And all I did was treat him like a person instead of a monster."

What about when you're being treated like a sub-human? Sometimes, the old switcheroo works under those circumstances, too. Marvin Corday is a clinical psychologist with a large practice in Southern California. In spite of his profession, however, Marvin used to have no better luck with consumer action than most of us do. He bought a watch, for instance, that conked out after only three weeks' wearing. "I wanted my money back, naturally," said Marvin. "So I took the watch down to the store, and the guy said I'd have to see the manager. The manager treated me like I was someone he'd just caught robbing the safe. I walked into his office, and he didn't even ask me to sit down. When I showed him the watch, he said I'd probably worn it in the shower, or something. I was about to start hollering at him, when I suddenly thought, hey, what would I do if this man were someone who'd come to see me, at my office, instead of the other way around?"

Instead of getting angry, Marvin calmly asked the manager of the store if there were anything wrong. After a moment of startled silence, the manager told him that, yes, there was. His young son was in the hospital with possible bone cancer, and the whole family was worried sick. For a few minutes, the manager told Marvin how upset his wife was, and how hard it was for them to face that their son might lose his arm and maybe even his life. When he was finished, he seemed much relieved. "You know," he told Marvin, "the least I can do after bending your ear like that is get you a watch that works. Or would you rather just have a credit with the store"? Marvin took the watch, which is still going strong some two years later. "Since then," says Marvin, "I always ask what's wrong if anybody treats me rudely or seems to want to start a fight. Nine times out of ten, there *is* a problem, and it has nothing to do with me or my complaint. Even the tenth case, the guy who just doesn't like my looks, is usually nicer after I've shown some consideration for him."

It would be pleasant to be able to say that the nice guy always finishes first, but of course, it wouldn't be true. It's surprising, though, how many consumer complaints can be expedited or even solved by the judicious use of a little human kindness. Now, suppose you're in a situation where extra consideration just won't do you any good. Suppose you've written three polite letters, made appointments and phone calls, all to no avail. Then what? Here's a strategy that got good results for an otherwise un-tricky woman named Marie Eggert. Marie moved into a middle-income housing project, the "base rents" of which were far higher than what most of the tenants were paying. The difference between a moderately-priced apartment and the rather inflated market rents that were nominally charged was made up by a subsidy from the federal government. So far, so good. But somehow, things didn't work out that way for Marie. When she had lived in the building a month, she paid her second month's rent -- the amount she could afford on the subsidy scale, and thought no more about it. In a week, she was faced with an angry-sounding computerized notice from the management. Her rent was late! According to the notice, she still owed a hundred dollars -- money which, according to Marie's lease, was supposed to be paid by a government grant.

At first, the whole affair didn't worry Marie very much. It was obviously some sort of office or computer error. After all, she had a written lease that stated the amount she was supposed to pay. She shot off a polite letter to the management company. Virtually by return mail, she got a very nasty letter, telling her that legal proceedings would be started against her if she didn't pay up. In the next few days, Marie telephoned the management office twelve times. Each time, she was only able to speak to a secretary or a clerk. Each time, she was told that the company's records showed she had agreed to pay the full market rent, not the subsidized rate. In the meantime, she got two more notices, saying that court action had already begun, and she could expect to be evicted soon. "The whole thing made me so nervous," she recalls. "I was making mistakes at work and crying all the time."

Finally, when all her attempts to get through to somebody with the authority to look into the errors had been frustrated, Marie got mad. It was then that her experiences as a reporter for her college newspaper came in useful. "I used to call lots of important people for interviews. You could almost always get to talk to the big boss by saying you worked for a newspaper. Of course, I never told them it was just the school paper until after I got them into the conversation." She decided that maybe the executive of the management firm who was always conveniently out to lunch or in a meeting might talk to a reporter, too. Just to make sure, she told the secretary that she worked for the biggest paper in town, and that she was investigating a report that the company cheated its moderate-income tenants by falsifying the leases after signing and trying to force the tenants to pay full market price.

This time, Marie was put through to the executive, who hotly denied the whole thing. "Well," said Marie, "we've had a report from a Ms. Eggert that this trick has been pulled on her, and she's willing to testify, if it should go to court."

"Just tell her to call me," said the executive with ingratiating smoothness. "I'm sure we can have the whole thing worked out before lunchtime." Marie made herself a cup of coffee and took care of a little paperwork she had been putting off. Then she called the management office again. Sure enough, the man had pulled her file and discovered a discrepancy between her lease and her computer records. He apologized to Marie, assuring her that she should keep paying the amount agreed on when the lease was signed. "Since then, I've used the reporter ploy a couple of times more," Marie confides. "Only now, if I have to do it, I get a friend of mine to call and be the reporter, usually a man. But I don't really think it would matter if they did know it was me. What counts is just getting the ear of that busy authority figure who's always hiding out from the ordinary complainer. Once you get hold of the people in charge, they're usually eager to make things right."

Which brings us to one of the biggest difficulties facing the consumer with a legitimate complaint: just how do you reach the supervisor or chief or vice president, whichever it may be, who can really do something about your problem? Marie Eggert's "reporter ploy" has more to recommend it than its dramatic aspects. Suppose you really were a reporter. Imagine that it's your job to reach the Big Chief and get the story from him, no matter what it takes. Sometimes a little method acting of this kind opens up new possibilities to you that you would never have thought of when you were just being yourself. You don't have to actually tell anyone that you're an investigative reporter or a hot-shot attorney, but just try to guess what you would do if you were. Then, go ahead and do it in behalf of yourself.

In the first place, any good reporter or lawyer would know the name of the person in charge, and the person above him, too. If you're being given the run-around by a hotel where you're supposed to have a room reserved, but which is suddenly all booked up, what can you do? One gesture that often works is to mention the name of the district manager, or the president of the company -- something like, "I wonder if Mr. Blank knows that you're overbooking and turning bona fide customers out without the rooms they were promised." Just the sound of Mr. Blank's name may make a room magically appear for you in the previously "full" hotel. It will be assumed that you are an associate or friend of Mr. (or Ms.) Blank, and that you should get some immediate attention or the boss will be raising some dust.

But, you say, I don't know any hotel chain vice presidents. Probably not. But you can still find out their names and keep the information in reserve in case you need it. Whenever you actually need to contact a V.I.P., the name is an absolute must. Usually, you can find out who you want to talk to just by calling the company switchboard and asking. If you feel awkward just calling up and saying, "Say, who's your vice president for consumer relations?" or "Who's in charge of public relations?" simply say that you're compiling a directory of such persons or -- the old standby -- that you're on the staff of a local paper and your editor wants the information. If you want to go even higher than the people officially designated to deal with your specific problem, you can find out the names of corporate officers and parent companies from business directories at the public library, or from the office of any stockbroker. If you think it's too much trouble to go all the way to the library to research a bit before you seek satisfaction, think again. In business, and especially in the world of interlocking corporations, names and titles open doors and connect phones.

As to just whose name will carry the most weight, it depends on the company, the complaint, and probably a lot of other factors that vary with the individual situation. In general, though, it never hurts to aim high, and it's a good idea to try for somebody who really cares what the public thinks of the company image. This is why it's sometimes more effective to contact the public relations department than it is to contact a department that is officially concerned with your area of complaint. Public relations workers (and presidents of companies) are directly interested in seeing that the organization retains the good will and trust of the buying public. If you even hint to such a person that you are so angry that you want to spread the word about the unreliability of the Standard Steam Iron, you will probably receive, at the very least, the offer of a new iron, if not someone to do the ironing for you.

George Dorchek is a man who knows the value of good publicity. He makes his living in advertising, and has made it his business to know what image can and cannot do for a product. Whenever George has a consumer complaint, he makes sure to find a responsible person to complain to, and he makes sure that the person knows what line of work George is in. There is always the implied threat -- all very low-key -- that George is prepared to provide the company with some bad publicity if his demands are not satisfied. Usually, the implied threat is enough to get action, but now and then something more explicit is required. Take the time George's office transferred him to the West Coast. Since he had to leave on short notice, without time to rent or buy a new house, George called a national moving and storage company and asked that his belongings be picked up and stored for him in California until he found a place to live. He was told that his things would be waiting for him on the Coast, and that as soon as he was ready, they would be delivered to his new house.

As luck would have it, George found a house he liked within a week of his arrival in California. He and his wife arranged to buy the house, which was already vacant, and called the moving company. George was told that his household goods were "still on the truck," and that they would arrive within the week. Meantime, George's family was virtually camping out in the new house, reluctant to buy anything new, since their own things were due to arrive any day. Two weeks went by in this fashion, then three. Each time George called the moving company, there was a new excuse: there had been delays in shipping; the Dorchek's things had been sent to Northern California by mistake; the clerk was unable to locate George's things, which had perhaps been put in the wrong warehouse. At the end of three weeks, George was convinced the company was giving him the run-around. Once he thought it was justified, George brought out the big guns. In his business directory, he found the name of the vice president in charge of public relations. As soon as he was put through, George began to explain his position in a calm, quiet voice.

"Mr. Evans," said George, "my name is George Dorchek. I want to tell you what I'm going to do for the next few weeks. I am going to make it a point, every day, to call people and organizations I know and tell them not to use your company for their moving needs. Since I know quite a few people, and they move around a lot, I don't suppose it will be too long until I've lost your company about a thousand dollars worth of business. When I have, I'll quit for the day. I plan to do this every day that you don't deliver my belongings as you said you would. That's what I'm going to do. Now, perhaps you'd like to tell me what you're going to do."

After a moment's stunned silence, the man at the other end of the line said, "I think what I'm going to do is find your stuff and see that it's at your house tomorrow." Sure enough, within twenty-four hours, the Dorchek furnishings had been "un-lost" and transferred to the Dorchek's new house.

Part of the success of consumer strategies like George Dorchek's lies in the manner assumed by the complainant. One must be determined to carry out whatever threat one makes to the company's image, and one must <u>seem</u> to be determined. This incident is not the first, or probably the last time that George has resorted to an attack on the good name of a firm in order to enforce his rights as a consumer. But, he cautions, such threats should never be made lightly or in a hysterical manner. "Never threaten to do something so far out that you would never carry through," he says. "You have to be sure it's something you'll really do, if you have to." If you plan to use such a strategy, it is vital that you voice your complaint to the right person. A dispatcher with a weekly paycheck doesn't care very much if you and your friends think he works for a great moving company or not. The people who care are those whose prosperity depends on the goodwill of the public, <u>and who know it</u>. This includes not only those who work in the public relations department, but all the high officers of the corporation (the higher the better) and people whose job it is to manage the advertising and public image of specific products. The higher up you go with your complaint, the more likely you are to reach someone to whom the firm's public-service image is important. Lower-echelon workers are usually not directly involved with the moral position of their employer vis-a-vis society, but company officers often care a great deal about not being -- and not being seen to be -- a bad guy.

Another feature of George Dorchek's style is worth noticing. Whenever he calls a company with a complaint, he has an exact idea of just what he wants that company to do for him. If the problem is defective merchandise, George never just crabs about it. "It doesn't tell them anything they can act on to say, 'the toaster you sold me won't toast,'" George says. "You have to explain, in detail, what you want them to do about it. But once you make your mind up about what will satisfy you, don't settle for less. If they've repaired the thing three times and it still won't work, don't let them talk you into another repair job. If you want a new toaster, insist on that. Or maybe you want your money back. Whatever it is, make sure they know what will satisfy you and what won't."

George Dorchek's principle of specific demands has wide application in the field of consumerism. The more exactly you can spell out what you want, the more likely you are to get it. Kathleen Heany is another careful consumer, buyer, and household manager who knows the value of having a specific goal in mind when you voice a complaint. Kathleen recently made a long trip from her home to a suburban shopping center to take advantage of a sale on spring suits. When she got to the store, she found that the sale suits were not at all like the ones in the full-page ad she had clipped from her morning paper. "I know that store very well," she says. "I go to the one near my house all the time, because they often have good, unadvertised sales. The suits in the photograph really were carried by the store, and they're excellent quality. But the sale suits were cheaper fabric and poorly cut. I suppose they thought nobody would know the difference. But I did." Kathleen insisted, first to the sales clerk and then to the manager of the department, that she wanted a suit like the ones in the photograph, and she wanted it at the sale price. Both store employees said that there was nothing they could do about it, they merely sold what the buying department told them to sell. But Kathleen was not about to give up. "Besides really wanting that suit, I thought they'd done something unfair. The suits in the ad looked much better than any of the sale merchandise could, just because they were much better made. A lot of consumers might be influenced by the image in the ad, buy the suit, and wonder why it never seemed to look right on them. I thought if the store could put those clothes in its ad, those were the clothes it should sell."

Kathleen was finally referred to the buyer for the department, who told her she could have any of the stock on the floor reduced to sale price. Still insistent, Kathleen said she wanted one of the suits represented in the ad, which she knew the store carried at some of its other branches. "Either that," she said sweetly, "or somebody should take an ad in the same paper telling people that you won't really sell what you advertised." After a further chat with the assistant director of merchandising for the whole chain of stores, Kathleen was told to go to her local branch and pick up one of the suits she wanted -- at the sale price. The full-page ad announcing the big suit sale did not run again.

If you think that a person must be either an actress or an extrovert to do what Kathleen Heany did, think again. Kathleen is a tiny, shy woman whose stage experience is limited to designing scenery for the local amateur group, and who tends to blush when spoken to by strangers. "It's not that I really like to make a fuss over things," she confides. "In fact, I'd much rather not. But I've been shy all my life, and I've found out that if you let people take advantage of you, they often will. Of you, and of others, too. I usually don't complain unless I think real harm is being done. With the suit, for instance. If it had just been that they didn't have the kind of thing I wanted on sale, I'd have turned around and gone home. But it was the fact that they falsified that ad that got to me. I thought that was a form of cheating, and that they ought to be stopped. When I think I'm acting in the public interest, I have the courage to do a lot of things I'd never do just for myself."

As a matter of fact, any time a merchant sells you a defective item, or otherwise misleads you, it *is* in the public interest to set the matter straight. If a company thinks the public doesn't much care whether they deliver on time or a week late or whether they call a product an FM-AM radio when only the AM service works, they can scarcely be blamed if they don't try very hard to get these things just right. If, on the other hand, the public complains about such things, the people who provide our goods and services will be more likely to think that attention to these "details" is part of their job. There is much talk these days about the decline of craftsmanship, the rise of worker apathy. "Nobody really cares if they do a good job or not anymore," one hears. Perhaps this is partly because nobody for whom the jobs are done seems to care very much.

Not everyone wants to set himself or herself up as a consumer advocate, especially when they have no particular interest in the outcome. But many people are so shy about complaining that they fail to get what's coming to them when their interests *are* at stake. Next time you find a filthy washroom in a gas station or see torn and soiled merchandise on a rack, speak up. Just mention, politely and pleasantly, that the establishment really should do something about that problem you've noticed. Besides doing a bit to make travelling or shopping more pleasant for the next person, you'll be putting in a little practice, getting in shape for the times -- and there are sure to be some -- when your complaints and their outcomes will really be important to you.

One final case history. You may not ever want to go to the extremes of action taken by a woman we will simply call Joan, but her case will give you an idea of what consumers can and will do when pushed to the limit. Joan moved into her new apartment on a Tuesday. On Wednesday, a man came to the door, saying he wanted to read the meter. When Joan let him in, all unsuspecting, he went down into the basement of the building (the only access was through her apartment) and removed the meter from the wall. When she saw him carrying the box out of the house, Joan asked him what he was doing. "Listen, lady," said the meter reader, "if you don't pay, you don't get lights."

Joan immediately got on the phone and called the utility, but they would only tell her that their records showed months of unpaid bills at her address. "But they're not _my_ bills," Joan cried. "I just moved in here yesterday"! Finally, she managed to reach a supervisor, who told her that he was very sorry for the mix-up, but that it would now take three weeks or so to set the matter straight. Meantime, alas, Joan would have to make do with candles. As you might imagine, Joan was furious. She bought a camping lantern and sat in her new apartment, brooding by the unfriendly light. In the morning, she was still furious, but she had a plan. She went to the branch library near her office and found out the name of the chairman of the utility. Then she went back to the office and looked him up in the phone book, but he was not listed. Undaunted, Joan called the chairman's office. "Oh," she was told, "Mr. Muchness has left for the weekend."

"That's terrible," wailed Joan into the phone. "I have to do a report for school, and it's supposed to be finished by Monday. I never thought he'd leave work so early."

"What a shame," said the sympathetic secretary. "But maybe if you call him at home and tell him your problem, he could find some time to talk to you this weekend."

Exactly what I was thinking, said Joan to herself as she copied down the chairman's suburban phone number. She did not dial the number right away. She waited, in fact, until one o'clock the next morning. Then, by the light of her camping lantern, she carefully called the number. After many rings, the chairman himself answered the phone.

"Mr. Muchness?" said Joan. "I was just sitting here at my office, and I thought I'd give you a call."

"Who the hell is this?" yelled Mr. Muchness.

"My name is Joan, Mr. Muchness. And I wanted to tell you why I have to be at my office at this hour of the morning. It's because I don't have any lights in my apartment, Mr. Muchness. Your company tells me it'll be three weeks until they can get around to putting my service back in. So I was just thinking, since I have to work late anyway, maybe I'll just give you a call every morning about this time, to see how you're coming with my lights."

After a little while, the chairman was calm enough to take Joan's full name and address. Just after eight the next morning, a Saturday, two workmen arrived at Joan's door to restore her service. While this is not necessarily recommended as a technique, it may serve as a cautionary tale. Never underestimate the power of a consumer wronged!

Chapter 4:
STATE CONSUMER AGENCIES

Consumer protection is a fairly new service for state governments to provide. In the past, the quality of service consumers could expect from the state depended largely on the personality and inclinations of the state's Attorney General. In many areas, the State's Attorney still handles consumer complaints, while other states have set up separate departments of consumer protection. In either case, the services have been considerably changed from the old hit-or-miss aid most people received back in the '40's and '50's. Consumer protection is now recognized as a legitimate and serious area of law, and an appropriate service for government to provide its citizens.

Consumer protection agencies are the government's watchdog on unfair or shoddy business practices. Any citizen who suspects he or she has been cheated in any way by a firm doing business in the state has the right to complain to the agency, and the right to expect his or her claim to be investigated. Most agencies do more than investigate. They try to work out a solution to the problem between the merchant and the consumer. When you have a complaint, call the office nearest you, whether it's the main office or a branch. Branch offices usually can do everything the main office can, or if not, they'll tell you whom to contact for more specialized services.

In this chapter, we will discuss state consumer agencies. A listing of state agencies and their branches (if any) is provided, arranged alphabetically. Whenever possible, you will find any additional services these agencies may provide to help the consumer. These services include toll-free numbers and helpful booklets. State agencies are funded by your tax dollars and as such should be a major source of help with your complaints, but keep in mind that they can only help with complaints on consumer problems arising within the state. The quality of consumer protection varies from state to state, and included here will be a success rate for each agency, if that information is available. Also, the top three or four areas of complaints are listed for your convenience. If you have failed to get satisfaction with your complaint on a local level, or if your state does not provide consumer protection organizations on a local level, this chapter will be of great help to you.

ALABAMA

Alabama provides two state consumer protection agencies. A toll-free hotline is available for calls from anywhere within the state. The number is 1-800-392-5658. Complaints usually take about four weeks for handling, and the agency is able to satisfactorily resolve approximately 40 percent of the complaints it receives. The addresses for these agencies are as follows:

Governor's Office of
  Consumer Protection
138 Adams Avenue
Montgomery, Alabama 36310
(205) 832-5936

Consumer Services Coordinator
Office of Attorney General
669 South Lawrence Street
Montgomery, Alabama 36107
(205) 832-6820

ALASKA

The Consumer Protection Section of the Attorney General's Office is the only full-time consumer protection office in the state of Alaska. It does not have a large staff or budget as yet, but what with the influx of new people because of the oil pipeline, it is hoped that this will soon change. Small as it is, it does provide the consumer with a valuable packet of information in the form of a "Consumer Protection Kit," which is available on request at the address below. This kit lists any agencies that can help you with a specialized complaint.

Assistant Attorney General
Chief Consumer Protection Section
Office of Attorney General
360 "K" Street
Anchorage, Alaska 99501
(907) 279-1567

Branch Offices
Pouch K
Juneau, Alaska 99801
(907) 586-5931

604 Barnette, Box 1309
Fairbanks, Alaska 99701
(907) 452-1567

ARIZONA

The three major areas of complaints in Arizona are mobile homes, automobile repairs and sales, and credit problems. Arizona requires that all consumer complaints be made in writing, and the average time taken to process a complaint is six to eight weeks. There were no figures available pertaining to their success rate. The address to write is as follows.

Chief Counsel
Economic Protection Division
Department of Law
159 State Capitol Building
Phoenix, Arizona 85007
(602) 271-5763

ARKANSAS

Arkansas has a statewide toll-free telephone number (1-800-482-8982) which is always a useful service. The majority of complaints in this state deal with automobile sales and repairs, magazines, home improvements and repairs, and mobile homes. Here is where to write:

Consumer Counsel
Consumer Protection Division
Office of Attorney General
Justice Building
Little Rock, Arkansas 72201
(501) 371-2341

Deputy Commissioner/Chief Counsel
Consumer Service Division
University Tower Building
12th and University, 400-18
Little Rock, Arkansas 72204
(501) 371-1325

CALIFORNIA

California is a very consumer conscious state and there are many laws on the books that protect the consumer. They have a unique way of handling complaints in this state. When the Department of Consumer Affairs is contacted with a complaint, they will refer it to any one of the thirty-six boards and bureaus designed to deal with different businesses and professions. If none of these boards or bureaus can be of help with your complaint, the Consumer Services Division will handle it. The Department of Consumer Affairs also publishes a good-sized booklet which lists the more than 180 laws recently passed dealing with consumer protection. This booklet is available on request. The major areas of consumer complaints for this state are landlord-tenant problems, auto sales and repairs, and mobile homes. California provides a toll-free number that is set up to deal specifically with auto repair complaints. This number is 1-800-952-5210. The addresses of the state agency and its branch offices are listed below.

Department of Consumer Affairs
1020 N Street
Sacramento, California 95814
(916) 445-1254

Branch Offices
107 South Broadway, Room 8020
Los Angeles, California 90012
(213) 620-2003

30 Van Ness Avenue, Room 2100
San Francisco, California 94102
(415) 557-2046

Deputy Attorney General
Environment/Consumer Protection
  Section
Office of Attorney General
350 McAllister Street
(800) 952-5225 (consumer
  complaints in California)

(916) 952-5225 (consumer
  complaints from out of state)

Consumer Affairs Division
Department of Insurance
600 South Commonwealth Avenue
Los Angeles, California 90005
(213) 620-4639 (insurance only)

1407 Market Street
San Francisco, California 94103
(415) 557-3646

COLORADO

Here are the major complaint areas being handled in this state: automobile sales and repairs, mail-order and publication-subscription problems, and home improvement problems. About forty percent of the cases handled are settled to the consumer's satisfaction, but the time taken to do so is generally about four weeks. There are two state offices that handle consumer complaints. The addresses and phone numbers are listed below.

Assistant Attorney General
Office of Consumer Affairs
Office of Attorney General
104 State Capitol
Denver, Colorado 80203
(303) 897-2542

Consumer and Food Specialist
Colorado Department of Agriculture
1525 Sherman Street, Room 422
Denver, Colorado 80203
(303) 892-3561

CONNECTICUT

There is good news for the consumer in Connecticut, for this state has a broad statute which prohibits deceptive and unfair trade practices. They also provide a toll-free number: 800-842-2649. Complaints take about three to six weeks to be processed, but figures for success rates were not available. Another helpful service is the free booklet called $ HELP $ provided by the Department of Consumer Protection for the asking. This booklet includes information on credit, purchasing, warranties, and what agencies are available for particular types of complaints. Below are the addresses and phone numbers where you can contact them.

Department of Consumer Protection
State Office Building
Hartford, Connecticut 06115
(203) 566-4999

Assistant Attorney General for
 Consumer Protection
Office of Attorney General
Room 177 - State Office Building
Hartford, Connecticut 06115
(203) 566-3035

Consumer Counsel
Office of Consumer Counsel
Connecticut Public Utility Commission
165 Capitol Avenue
State Office Building
Hartford, Connecticut 06115
(203) 506-7287

DELAWARE

The two main areas of complaint in this state are problems that have to do with dwellings and home furnishings. Delaware is quite good at handling their consumers' complaints, with a success rate of well over seventy percent. For those of you who don't live in the state capital, the Division of Consumer Affairs provides the convenience of local telephone numbers in three counties. When a call is made on the local number, it is put through directly to Wilmington. The numbers are: New Castle County, 571-3250; Kent County, 678-4000; and Sussex County, 856-2571. The numbers are particularly useful since the Delaware Division of Consumer Affairs is one of those states that does not require a complaint in writing, and is willing to handle complaints informally over the phone whenever possible. If you do have occasion to write to them, here are the addresses:

Consumer Affairs Division
Department of Community Affairs
 and Economic Development
200 W. Ninth St., 6th Floor
Wilmington, Delaware 19801
(302) 571-3250

Deputy Attorney General
Consumer Protection Division
Department of Justice
Public Building
Wilmington, Delaware 19801
(302) 571-2524

DISTRICT OF COLUMBIA

The District of Columbia is fairly efficient in handling its consumer complaints, with the average waiting period only about a week. The rate of success of complaints handled is about seventy-five percent. Most of their complaints seem to concern television, appliance, and electronic repairs, home improvement repairs, and auto sales and repairs. To write to them, use the addresses below.

Director
D.C. Office of Consumer Affairs
1407 "L" Street
Washington, D.C. 20005
(202) 629-2617

Office of the People's Counsel
  of the District of Columbia
1625 "I" Street, N.W.
Washington, D.C. 20006
(202) 727-3071

FLORIDA

Condominiums are at the top of Florida's complaint list, followed by land sales, auto complaints, and mobile homes. A toll-free number (1-800-342-2176) is provided for your convenience. Many of Florida's agencies handle only specific complaints. The listing below makes a note of these specific areas, so you will know whom to contact with what complaint. If there is no listing for your complaint, just contact the branch office nearest you for help.

Counsel, Consumer Protection
  and Fair Trade Practices Bureau
Department of Legal Affairs
State Capitol
Tallahassee, Florida 32304
(904) 488-4481

Branch Offices
Assistant Attorney General
Sunset Executive Center
8585 Sunset Dr. - Suite 75
Miami, Florida 33143
(305) 279-8700

Assistant Attorney General
419 Stoval Professional Bldg.
305 Morgan Street
Tampa, Florida 33602
(813) 223-3561

Director
Division of Consumer Services
Department of Agriculture and
  Consumer Services
107 Mayo Building
Tallahassee, Florida 32304
(904) 488-2221

Director for Consumer Protection
Office of the Comptroller
State Capitol
Tallahassee, Florida 32304
(904) 488-5275 or 488-8830

Branch Offices
1515 N.W. 7th St. - Room 210
Miami, Florida 33125
(305) 649-8650

103 Century Twenty-One Drive
Suite 113
Jacksonville, Florida 32216
(904) 724-3952

807 W. Morse Blvd. - Suite 201
Winter Park, Florida 32789
(305) 644-4353

Executive Square Office Park
Suite 113, 402 Rio St.
Tampa, Florida 33602
(813) 272-2565

2453 N. Military Trail
West Palm Beach, Florida 33401
(305) 686-8640

880 N. Reus St., Suite 5A
Pensacola, Florida 32501
(904) 434-0626

Chief
Bureau of Consumer Research and
  Education
Department of Insurance
State Capitol, Suite 53
Tallahassee, Florida 32304
(904) 488-6084 (insurance only)

Branch Offices
(For the service office nearest
 you, call (904) 488-6085)

Director
Office of Consumer Affairs
Public Service Commission
780 South Adams St.
Tallahassee, Florida 32304
(904) 488-7238
1-800-342-3552 (for utility complaints only)

Public Counsel
Office of Public Counsel
Holland Bldg., Room 308
Tallahassee, Florida 32304
(904) 488-9330 (litigation only)

GEORGIA

Georgia has a truly enlighted system for handling consumer complaints. They have a toll-free number, 1-800-282-4900, which is called the Tie-Line. If your complaint would best be handled by another agency, you are immediately connected with the person in that agency that you need to talk to. Tie-Line calls are taken by trained counselors who will either connect you with the agency you need, or help you to solve your problem by making a quick phone call (if possible) while you wait. If they cannot help in either of these two ways, they will write down your complaint and resolve it within twenty-four hours. About three-quarters of the complaints handled are resolved in this way, and those that aren't handled within twenty-four hours are usually solved in about a week. This gives Georgia a success rate of about eighty percent. If you do need to write, the addresses are below.

Administrator
Governor's Office of Consumer Affairs
104 State Capitol
Atlanta, Georgia 30334
(404) 656-1794

Assistant Attorney General for
  Deceptive Practices
Office of Attorney General
132 State Judicial Building
Atlanta, Georgia 30334
(404) 656-3343

Wheeler Bryan
Consumers' Utility Counsel of
  Georgia
c/o Bryan, Ramos and Arnold
134 Peachtree St.
310 Rhodes Haverty Building
Atlanta, Georgia 30303
(404) 681-0444 (on state re-
  tainer basis)

HAWAII

The Office of Consumer Protection is the only broad-based consumer protection agency in the state of Hawaii. However, their success rate is quite impressive, with no less than eighty-five percent of their cases handled satisfactorily, though it may take up to eight weeks to process a complaint. Car problems and landlord-tenant disputes are the two major areas of consumer complaints. The Office for Consumer Complaints does have some impressive powers. When a company is the object of consumer complaints, the OCP can secure an 'assurance of voluntary conpliance' from that company. It can also get them to agree, in writing, to reimburse the consumer for the problems caused. The OCP, in effect, becomes the consumer's bargaining agent. Here is how to get in touch with them.

Director of Consumer Protection
Office of the Governor
250 S. King St.
602 Kamamalu Bldg.
P.O. Box 3767
Honolulu, Hawaii 96811
(808) 548-2560 (administration)
(808) 548-2540 (complaints)

IDAHO

Food and drugs, automobile sales and repairs, and mobile homes are what the Consumer Protection Division in Idaho hear the most about. There is no toll-free number for this state agency, and it is probably best to submit complaints to them in writing. Although they don't have a toll-free number, they do have two publications that are of value to the consumer. The first provides a list of useful state and federal laws. This publication, the Consumer-Business Relations in Idaho, is free on request. The other, Idaho Consumer News, is the Consumer Division's monthly newsletter. This will give you handy tips on buying, and national as well as local consumer news of importance. This is also free to state residents. There are no figures available concerning success rates or waiting periods for the state. Write to:

Deputy Attorney General
Consumer Protection Division
Office of the Attorney General
State Capitol, Room 225
Boise, Idaho 83720
(208) 384-2400

ILLINOIS

Illinois has two separate consumer protection agencies on the state level, each with its own branch offices. The one run by the attorney general's office has a success rate of over sixty-five percent and a waiting period of two to three weeks. A success rate for the agency run by the governor's office was unavailable, but the waiting period for complaints is usually less than two weeks. Both agencies list automobile problems as the number one area of complaint. Complaints about home improvements followed as a close second, particularly with regards to waterproofing firms. Complaints about mail-order houses ranked third. Both offices would prefer complaints to be made in writing, so check the addresses below for the office nearest you.

Consumer Advocate's Office
Office of the Governor
State of Illinois Bldg.
160 N. LaSalle St. - Room 2000
Chicago, Illinois 60601
(312) 793-2754

Assistant Attorney General and
 Chief, Consumer Fraud Section
Office of the Attorney General
134 N. LaSalle St. - Room 204
Chicago, Illinois 60602
(312) 793-3580

Branch Offices
Special Assistant to the Attorney
 General
2151 Madison-Project Uplift
Bellwood, Illinois 60104
(No Telephone)

Special Assistant to the Attorney
 General
13051 Greenwood Ave.
Blue Island, Illinois 60406
(313) 597-8984

Special Assistant to the Attorney
 General
50 Raupp Blvd.
Buffalo Grove, Illinois 60090
(312) 537-8984

Special Assistant to the Attorney
 General
1104 N. Ashland Ave.
Chicago, Illinois 60622
(312) 793-5638

Special Assistant to the Attorney
 General
7906 S. Cottage Grove
Chicago, Illinois 60619
(312) 488-2600

Special Assistant to the Attorney
 General
800 Lee St.
Des Plaines, Illinois 60016
(No Telephone)

Special Assistant to the Attorney
 General
901 Wellington St.
Elk Grove Village, Illinois 60007
(312) 439-3900

Special Assistant to the Attorney
 General
Evanston Library-1703 Orrington
Evanston, Illinois 60204
(312) 475-6700

Special Assistant to the Attorney
 General
71 N. Ottawa St.
Joliet, Illinois 60434
(815) 727-5371

Special Assistant to the Attorney
 General
1603 North Ave.
McHenry, Illinois 60050
(815) 384-1703

Special Assistant to the Attorney General
6300 N. Lincoln Ave.
Morton Grove, Illinois 60053
(312) 967-4100

Special Assistant to the Attorney General
217 S. Civic Dr.
Schaumberg, Illionis 60172
(312) 894-7771

Special Assistant to the Attorney General
5127 Oakton St.
Skokie, Illinois 60076
(312) 674-2522

Special Assistant to the Attorney General
149 S. Genesee
Waukegan, Illinois 60085
(312) 244-4900

Assistant Attorney and Chief Consumer Protection Division
Office of the Attorney General
500 South Second St.
Springfield, Illinois 62706
(217) 782-1090

Branch Offices
Special Assistant to the Attorney General
Alton Chamber of Commerce Bldg.
112 E. Broadway
Alton, Illinois 62002
(612) 462-9201

Special Assistant to the Attorney General
102 S. Washington, Suite 12
Carbondale, Illionis 62901
(618) 549-3369

Special Assistant to the Attorney General
820 Martin Luther King Dr.
East St. Louis, Illinois 62201
(618) 874-2238

Special Assistant to the Attorney General
Main St.
Peoria, Illinois 61602
(309) 772-3100

Special Assistant to the Attorney General
208 18th St.
Rock Island, Illinois 61201
(309) 786-3303

Special Assistant to the Attorney General
401 W. State St.
Rockford, Illinois 61101
(815) 965-8635

Special Assistant to the Attorney General
123 N. Garrard St.
Rantoul, Illinois 61866
(217) 893-1401

Deputy Director
Consumer Market Branch
Department of Insurance
215 E. Monroe
Springfield, Illinois 62767
(217) 782-4515 (insurance only)

INDIANA

Indiana provides two valuable services for its consumer. The first is a toll-free number for consumer complaints; 800-382-5516. The second is a booklet called Consumer Assistance Agencies in Indiana which is available free on request from the state Consumer Protection Division. This booklet will help you to find the right agency to contact with your complaint. Unlike so many states, auto complaints rank only third in Indiana. The two top areas of complaint in this state are door-to-door sales and mail-order houses. Figures for success rates and waiting periods were unavailable, but if you ask the agency when you write or call they may be able to give a rough estimate of how long it will take to process your complaint. Here's where to call or write.

Assistant Attorney General
Chief, Consumer Protection Division
Office of Attorney General
215 State House
Indianapolis, Indiana 46204
(317) 633-6496 or 633-6276

Deputy Commissioner & Director
Consumer Services Division
Department of Insurance
State Office Bldg. - Room 509
Indianapolis, Indiana 46204
(317) 633-6338 (insurance only)

Division of Consumer Credit
Department of Financial Institutions
1024 Indiana State Office Bldg.
Indianapolis, Indiana 46204
(317) 633-6297 (credit only)

Public Counselor
Office of Public Counselor
807 State Office Bldg.
Indianapolis, Indiana 46204
(317) 633-4659 (utilities only)

IOWA

The state consumer agency is the only governmental consumer protection in Iowa. They are quite efficient, with a success rate of no less than seventy percent, but it does take them four to six weeks to process a complaint. They do not have a toll-free number, and they request that all complaints be made to them in writing. The most common complaints in this state concern land sales, buying clubs, health spas, and trade and correspondence schools. The single address for the state agency is listed below.

Assistant Attorney General in Charge
Consumer Protection Division
Office of the Attorney General
1209 E. Court

Executive Hills West
Des Moines, Iowa 50319
(515) 218-5926

KANSAS

The Consumer Protection Division in Kansas estimates a success rate of eighty-five percent of all the complaints they receive. The average wait for processing a complaint is also very good -- only two weeks. As with so many states, the number one area for complaints is automobile sales and repairs. This 'old faithful' is followed by mobile homes and door-to-door sales. There is a state agency in Kansas that handles complaints that specifically have to do with insurance. Kansas has no toll-free number for its consumer complaints, so it is best to write them at the following addresses.

Assistant Attorney General and Chief
Consumer Protection Division
Office of Attorney General
State Capitol
Topeka, Kansas 66612
(913) 296-3751

Commissioner
State Insurance Department
State Office Bldg., Room 129-S
Topeka, Kansas 66612
(913) 296-3071
1-800-432-2484 (insurance only)

KENTUCKY

There is a toll-free number for Kentucky's Consumer Protection Division which is being well advertised by the state. The number is 1-800-372-2960. The success rate for this state is a little over seventy percent, but it can be a month or more before a complaint is processed. The Consumer Protection Division does put out two booklets that are available on request. One is called Kentucky's Consumer Protection Laws, which will help you to know your legal rights. The other booklet is titled Ten Danger Signals in Buying. The top three areas for complaint by consumers here in Kentucky are pretty much what they are for most of the nation: mail-order houses, automobile problems, and home improvement and repairs. Contact this state agency at:

Assistant Deputy Attorney General
Consumer Protection Division
State Capitol, Room 34
Frankfort, Kentucky 40601
(502) 564-6607

LOUISIANA

Louisiana has a toll-free number called the 'Public Assistance Line,' which will connect you with any state agency. Most of the calls received are for the Governor's Office of Consumer Protection (GOCP). The GOCP is willing to try and handle your problem over the phone or give you advice about how you can go about doing it yourself. If you still wish to make a formal complaint in writing, the agency will begin mediation with the business involved within seven days after they receive it. If your complaint is of an emergency nature, they will begin processing immediately whether you write or phone. In such a case it is often likely that a problem will be resolved within hours of the initial contact. When you consider that Louisiana has a success rate of over seventy-five percent, this short waiting period makes Louisiana one of the more efficient and outstanding states for the handling of the consumer's problems. The areas for many of the complaints here are household goods and services, retail stores and services, and motor vehicle repairs and sales. Here's where to get in touch with them.

Director
Governor's Office of Consumer
  Protection
1885 Wooddale Blvd., Room 1218
P.O. Box 44091, Capitol Station
Baton Rouge, Louisiana 70804
(504) 389-7483

Branch Office
Consumer Protection and
  Commercial Fraud Unit
106 Henry Beck Building
Shreveport, Louisiana 71101
(318) 425-7493

Southern Regional Director
Consumer Protection and Commercial
  Fraud Unit
234 Loyola Ave., 7th Floor
New Orleans, Louisiana 70112
(504) 527-8371

State Director
Consumer Protection Commercial
  Fraud Prosecution Unit
Office of Attorney General
1885 Wooddale Blvd., Room 1208
Baton Rouge, Louisiana 70806
(504) 389-7228

Assistant Director
Bureau of Marketing
Department of Agriculture
P.O. Box 44302, Capitol Station
Baton Rouge, Louisiana 70804
(504) 344-8506

MAINE

Maine has a success rate of more than seventy percent, and the waiting depends on how difficult a problem the state agency is asked to handle. The top complaint areas for this state are unauthorized charges for services and repairs, auto sales and repairs, and non-performance of warranties. This agency prefers that you submit your complaint in writing to one of the addresses listed below.

Assistant Attorney General
Division of Consumer Fraud
  and Protection
Office of Attorney General
State House
Augusta, Maine 04330
(207) 289-3716

Superintendent
Bureau of Consumer Protection/
  Consumer Credit
51 Chapel St.
Augusta, Maine 04330
(207) 289-3731 (credit, truth-
  in-lending, collection agencies)

Consumer Division
Bureau of Insurance
Department of Business Regulation
State Office Annex
Western Ave.
Augusta, Maine 04330
(207) 289-3141 (insurance only)

MARYLAND

Maryland has an interesting approach to helping consumers with their complaints. Every month, members of the Consumer Protection Division go to nine locations throughout the state, collect complaints, and give advice on consumer problems. Three of these locations, in Baltimore, specialize in helping people who are receiving social service funds. Other locations are: Fort Meade, Easton, Frederick, Woodlawn, Cumberland, and Salisbury. Major areas of concern for consumers in this state are home improvements, automobile repairs, and appliances. No figures were available as to Maryland's success rate for resolving complaints, or for the length of time needed to process a complaint. If you miss out on one of their 'traveling shows' (dates for these visits can be gotten from your local city hall, or from the Consumer Protection Division itself), you can contact the CDP at one of the following addresses.

Assistant Attorney General and Chief
Consumer Protection Division
Office of Attorney General
One South Calvert St.
Baltimore, Maryland 21202
(301) 383-3713

Branch Offices
Metro, Branch Office
Maryland Attorney General's
 Consumer Protection Division
5112 Berwyn Rd., 2nd Floor
College Park, Maryland 20740
(301) 474-3500

Western Maryland Branch Office
Maryland Attorney General's
 Consumer Protection Division
138 E. Antietam St.
Hagerstown, Maryland 21740
(301) 791-1150

Director
Dealer Licensing & Consumer
 Services
Motor Vehicle Administration
6601 Ritchie Hwy., N.E.
Glen Burnie, Maryland 21601
(301) 768-7420

People's Counsel
Public Service Commission
301 W. Preston St.
Baltimore, Maryland 21201
(301) 383-2375

Commissioner of Consumer Credit
One South Calvert St., Room 601
Baltimore, Maryland 21202
(301) 383-3656

MASSACHUSETTS

Massachusetts is one of the outstanding states for the defense of the rights of consumers; fully ninety-five percent of the complaints received by the Executive Office of Consumer Affairs are successfully resolved, and it usually takes them only about two weeks to process a complaint. The three top categories for the complaints they receive are mail-order houses, appliances, and, you guessed it, auto sales and repairs. The state agencies do prefer you to write so here are the addresses.

Secretary
Executive Office of Consumer Affairs
John W. McCormack Bldg.
One Ashburton Place
Boston, Massachusetts 02108
(617) 727-8000

Director
Consumer Complaint Division
John W. McCormack Bldg.
One Ashburton Place
Boston, Massachusetts 02108
(617) 727-7755

Chief
Consumer Protection Division
Department of Attorney General
State House, Room 167
Boston, Massachusetts 02133
(617) 727-8406

Branch Office
Assistant Attorney General
  for Consumer Protection
Office of Attorney General
235 Chestnut St.
Springfield, Massachusetts 01103
(413) 785-1951

Executive Secretary
Massachusetts Consumers'
  Council
Leverett Saltonstall Building
Government Center
100 Cambridge St., Room 2109
Boston, Massachusetts 02202
(617) 727-2603 or 2606

MICHIGAN

The success rate for the Michigan Consumer Protection/Antitrust Division is only about sixty percent, but it is hoped that in the future this percentage will increase, for the state legislature has declared war on Michigan's major consumer problem: cars. The average time to process a complaint is about a month, so patience is the password. Michigan does have a toll-free number, 1-800-292-2431, but unfortunately, it is only for complaints concerning land sales. So unless your problem has to do with land, your best bet is to write them at one of the following addresses.

Assistant Attorney General in Charge
Consumer Protection/Antitrust Div.
Office of Attorney General
670 Law Bldg.
Lansing, Michigan 48913
(517) 373-1140

Special Deputy Commissioner
Consumer Services Division
Insurance Bureau
Department of Commerce
111 N. Hosmer St.
Lansing, Michigan 48913
(517) 373-0220 (insurance only)

Executive Director
Michigan Consumer Council
414 Hollister Bldg.
Lansing, Michigan 48933
(517) 373-0947

MINNESOTA

Although Minnesota's state agency is not as large as that in many other states, it does have an important power. The Office of Consumer Services can act as a mediator in consumer disputes, and if necessary, it can secure court orders for restitution to consumers. Their success rate depends on the difficulty of the problem handled. For a simple problem, such as undelivered merchandise, their success rate is very close to one hundred percent. For a problem that has to do with autos or mobile homes, the rate drops to about forty percent. Not bad, but not good either. Major problems for Minnesota consumers seem to occur in the areas of unfair business practices, credit problems, and collection agencies. The average time to process a complaint is about five weeks. Since they don't have a toll-free 'hotline,' here's where to get in touch with them.

Assistant Attorney General
Consumer Protection Division
Office of Attorney General
102 State Capitol
St. Paul, Minnesota 55155
(612) 296-3353

Branch Office
Investigator
Duluth Regional Office
332 W. Superior Rd.
Duluth, Minnesota 55802
(218) 723-4891

Director
Office of Consumer Services
Department of Commerce
Metro Square Bldg., 5th Floor
7th & Roberts Streets
St. Paul, Minnesota 55101
(612) 296-4512

Commissioner of Insurance and
 Chairman of Commerce Commission
Consumer Advocacy Program
Metro Square Bldg., 5th Floor
St. Paul, Minnesota 55101
(612) 296-2488 (insurance matters only)

MISSISSIPPI

The Mississippi Legislature has given the Attorney General's Office, rather than a separate agency, the power to seek restitution for consumers through court orders against those firms who have done the consumer harm. The agency's success rate is also well over fifty percent, with the average time to handle a complaint about three or four weeks. Mobile homes, home repairs, and automobile sales and repairs head the list for complaints in this state. Below are the addresses and phone numbers where you can send your complaint.

Chief
Consumer Protection Division
Office of Attorney General
Justice Building
P. O. Box 220
Jackson, Mississippi 39205
(601) 354-7130

Consumer Protection Division
Department of Agriculture and Commerce
High and President Sts.
P. O. Box 1609
Jackson, Mississippi 39205
(601) 354-6586

MISSOURI

The success rate in Missouri is quite good, compared to many states, coming in at about seventy-five percent. This rate, combined with the surprisingly low waiting period of about ten days, makes the Consumer Affairs Division of the state of Missouri a good bet to go to with your consumer problem. If you are complaining about deceptive business practices, car problems, or home repairs, you'll be right in step with a lot of other Missourians, for these are the top three categories for consumer complaints. So step right up and look below for the address nearest you.

Chief Counsel
Consumer Protection Division
Office of Attorney General
Supreme Court Bldg., P.O. Box 899
Jefferson City, Missouri 65101
(314) 751-3321

Branch Offices
Consumer Protection Division
Office of Attorney General
705 Olive St., Suite 1323
St. Louis, Missouri 63101
(314) 241-2211

Consumer Protection Division
Office of Attorney General
615 E. 13th St.
Kansas City, Missouri 64106
(816) 274-6686

Director
Office of Consumer Services
Department of Consumer Affairs,
  Regulation and Licensing
P.O. Box 1157
Jefferson City, Missouri 65101
(314) 751-4996

Director
Division of Insurance
515 E. High St., Box 690
Jefferson City, Missouri 65101
(314) 751-4126

Branch Offices
615 E. 13th St.
Kansas City, Missouri 64106
(816) 274-6381

225 S. Meramec
St. Louis, Missouri 63105
(314) 863-7735

MONTANA

Montana's consumer protection agency is fairly new compared to other states, having been created in 1973. But what they lack in age, they make up in efficiency. The success rate for this state agency is eighty percent and action on a complaint only takes about two weeks. Congratulations, Montana! General categories for complaints follow national trends with auto repairs and appliance problems heading the list. Third on that list are problems with credit and credit bureaus. Since they don't have a toll-free number as yet, it is best to write your complaints and send them to one of the following addresses.

Administrator
Consumer Affairs Division
Department of Business Regulation
805 N. Main St.
Helena, Montana 59601
(406) 449-3163

Montana Consumer Counsel
330 Fuller Ave.
Helena, Montana 59601
(406) 449-2771 or 2772 (utility
  and transportation matters
  only)

NEBRASKA

There were no figures available for success rate or average waiting time on complaints. This may be because Nebraska's Consumer Protection Division is not very large, with a staff of less than ten people. However, it is always wise to leave no stone unturned when it comes to a consumer problem, so do try the state agency. You may be pleasantly surprised with their service.

Special Assistant Attorney General
Department of Justice
State Capitol, 10th Floor
Lincoln, Nebraska 68509
(402) 471-2682

Consumer Consultant
Consumer Division
Department of Agriculture
P.O.Box 94844
Lincoln, Nebraska 68509
(402) 471-2341

NEVADA

The Consumer Affairs Division has a toll-free number to help Nevada consumers get help fast. That number is 800-992-0900. If this division thinks your problem needs legal handling, it will send it on to Nevada's other state agency, the Consumer Protection Division, for prosecution. The success rate for these agencies is about ninety percent, with an average processing period of one to fourteen days for most cases. Food and drugs, auto repairs and sales, and complaints about furniture are at the top of the list of consumer problems in Nevada. Here are the addresses and phone numbers to use the next time you have a problem.

Deputy Attorney General
Consumer Affairs Division
Office of Attorney General
2501 E. Sahara Ave., 3rd Floor
Las Vegas, Nevada 89104
(702) 385-0344

Commissioner
Consumer Affairs Division
Department of Commerce
Bradley Bldg., 3rd Floor
2501 E. Sahara Ave.
Las Vegas, Nevada 89104
(702) 385-0344

NEW HAMPSHIRE

If you live in this state and have a problem connected with land sales, you're in luck. The state's consumer protection agency can hear your complaint and work to resolve it in a way that resembles a legal court. New Hampshire's agency can also claim a success rate of more than seventy percent, with a waiting period for action on a complaint of about six weeks. The three areas where the most complaints are heard are mail-order houses, automobile sales and repairs, and home improvements. The address for this agency is:

Chief
Consumer Protection Division
Office of Attorney General
Statehouse Annex
Concord, New Hampshire 03301
(603) 271-3641

NEW JERSEY

New Jersey has a unique program initiated by their state Office of Consumer Affairs. It is called the CALA ("Community Affairs Local Assistance") program, and its purpose is to put a consumer officer in as many communities as possible in order to reach as many consumers with problems as possible. The CALA officer will try to handle your problem him- or herself, but if this is not possible, then the complaint will be forwarded to the central office of Consumer Affairs in Newark. The officer will keep you posted on the progress of your complaint, and will also give you advice on any other consumer problems you may have. At last count, there were over 125 CALA officers in the state of New Jersey. Your local city hall will be able to tell you if there is one in your home town, or where to reach the one closest to where you live. If the CALA officer can't handle your complaint, or if there is no CALA representative conveniently near to you, then you will need to send your complaint in writing to one of the addresses listed below. As with so many other states, the top complaint category in New Jersey is auto repairs and sales, closely followed by appliances, and home repairs and improvements. It usually takes two to four weeks to process a complaint, and the success rate is about sixty percent. If you have a complaint about a state agency that has mistreated you, New Jersey also has a department for that. Get in touch with the Division of Citizen Complaints & Dispute Settlement, Department of Public Advocate, P.O.Box 141, Trenton, New Jersey 08625. This particular state agency has its own toll-free number (800-792-8600), which seems to show that they really want to know if you are being mistreated by your own state government. New Jersey should be commended for their concern with the problems of the consumer in that state.

Director
Division of Consumer Affairs
Department of Law and Public Safety
1101 Raymond Blvd., Room 504
Newark, New Jersey 07102
(201) 648-4010

Assistant Attorney General
Division of Law
Department of Law and Public Safety
1100 Raymond Blvd., Room 316
Newark, New Jersey 07102
(201) 648-2478

Director of CALA Program
Division of Consumer Affairs
Department of Law and Public Safety
1100 Raymond Blvd., Room 504
Newark, New Jersey 07102
(201) 648-3559

Director of Consumer Services
Department of Insurance
201 E. State St.
Trenton, New Jersey 08625
(609) 292-5363

NEW MEXICO

New Mexico's success rate is about fifty percent, and it takes at least four weeks for a complaint to be processed. The general areas of complaint for this state are mobile home parks, mail-order houses, and auto repairs. There is only one address for the state.

Director
Consumer Protection Division
Office of Attorney General

P.O.Box 2246
Santa Fe, New Mexico 87501
(505) 827-2844 or 5237

NEW YORK

In New York, the mainstay of consumer protection is the Consumer Frauds and Protection Bureau. They prefer that you send them your complaints in writing. Though figures for a success rate were not available, you can be fairly certain that they are good. The Bureau has many legal powers, a large staff that includes investigators and lawyers, and a budget of at least $1 million. New Yorkers are complaining primarily about credit problems, automobile sales and repairs, and mail-order houses. The state agencies have branch offices all over the state, so check the listing below for the one nearest you.

Chairman and Executive Director
Consumer Protection Board
99 Washington Ave., Room 1000
Albany, New York 12210
(518) 474-8583

Branch Office
Two World Trade Center
Room 8225, 82nd Floor
New York, New York 10047
(212) 488-5666

Assistant Attorney General in Charge
Consumer Frauds and Protection
 Bureau
Office of Attorney General
Two World Trade Center
New York, New York 10047
(212) 488-7530

Assistant Attorney General in Charge
Consumer Frauds and Protection
 Bureau
Office of Attorney General
State Capitol
Albany, New York 12224
(518) 474-8686

Branch Offices of the Attorney
General's Consumer Frauds and
Protection Bureau

Assistant Attorney General in
 Charge
Office of Attorney General
403 Metcalf Bldg.
Auburn, New York 13021
(315) 253-9765

Assistant Attorney General in
 Charge
Office of Attorney General
19 Chenango St.
Binghamton, New York 13901
(607) 773-7823

Assistant Attorney General in
 Charge
Office of Attorney General
48 Cornelia St.
Plattsburgh, New York 12901
(518) 561-1980

Assistant Attorney General in
 Charge
Office of Attorney General
65 Broad St.
Rochester, New York 14614
(714) 454-4540

Assistant Attorney General in
 Charge
Office of Attorney General
333 E. Washington St.
Syracuse, New York 13202
(315) 473-8439, Ext. 216

Assistant Attorney General in Charge
Office of Attorney General
2 Catherine St.
Poughkeepsie, New York 14301
(914) 452-7760

Assistant Attorney General in Charge
Office of Attorney General
207 Genesse St., Box 258
Utica, New York 13501
(315) 797-6120

Assistant Attorney General in Charge
Office Attorney General
317 Washington St.
Watertown, New York 13001
(315) 782-0100

Chief
Consumer Complaint Bureau
State Insurance Department
Two World Trade Center
New York, New York 10047
(212) 488-4005
(insurance only)

Branch Office
Supervisor
Consumer Complaint Bureau
State Insurance Department
Albany, New York 12210
(518) 474-4556
(insurance only)

NORTH CAROLINA

The Consumer Protection Division of North Carolina can mediate on your behalf with the business causing the complaint, and if necessary they can prosecute. They have a toll-free 'hot-line' for your convenience; 1-800-662-7925. Their success is about seventy percent, although complaints generally take a month or two to be processed. Problems with mobile homes are at the head of their complaint list, along with undelivered merchandise, and auto sales and repairs. Here are the addresses and phone numbers where you can contact them.

Assistant Attorney General and
  Division Head
Consumer Protection Division
Office of Attorney General
Justice Bldg.
P.O. Box 629
Raleigh, North Carolina 27602
(919) 829-7741

Special Assistant for Consumer
  Affairs
Administration Division
Department of Insurance
Wake County Courthouse
316 Fayetteville St.
Raleigh, North Carolina 27611
(919) 829-2032
1-800-662-7975 (insurance only)

Assistant Commissioner and Director
Office of Consumer Services
Department of Agriculture
P.O. Box 27647
Raleigh, North Carolina 27611
(919) 829-7125

NORTH DAKOTA

The state consumer agency is the only game in town for residents of North Dakota. There are no county or local consumer agencies there. However, the good news is that they appear to be a highly efficient organization, with a success rate of over ninety-five percent. The average time for processing a complaint is about a month. The Consumer Affairs Office also offers a free monthly newsletter called <u>North Dakota Consumer</u>. It provides state-wide consumer news, plus helpful tips on protecting your rights as a consumer. The major complaints in this state are with mobile home, appliance, and automobile problems.

Assistant Attorney General and Counsel
Consumer Fraud Division
Office of Attorney General
State Capitol
Bismark, North Dakota 58501
(701) 224-2210

Consumer Specialist
Consumer Affairs Office
State Laboratories Department
Bank of North Dakota Bldg., Box 937
Bismark, North Dakota 58505
(701) 224-2485

Commissioner
Claims Division
North Dakota Insurance Dept.
Capitol Bldg.
Bismark, North Dakota 58505
(701) 224-2440 or 2451
(insurance only)

OHIO

Ohio residents have a toll-free number to call their state agency with their complaints. That number is 800-282-1960. The majority of complaints received by this state concern housewares and appliances, auto repairs and sales, and mail-order houses. This state has two separate state agencies to handle consumer complaints, the Consumer Protection Division and the Consumer Frauds and Crimes Section; they have a success rate of about eighty percent.

Assistant Attorney General and
  Section Chief
Consumer Frauds and Crimes Section
Office of Attorney General
State Office Tower, Suite 1541
30 E. Broad St.
Columbus, Ohio 43215
(614) 466-8831

Chief
Consumer Protection Division
Department of Commerce
180 E. Broad St., 13th Floor
Columbus, Ohio 43215
(614) 466-8760
(800) 282-1960 (all calls except
  real estate and insurance)

OKLAHOMA

Oklahoma also has two state agencies to help you. One is the Consumer Protection Division of the Attorney General's Office, and the other is the Department of Consumer Affairs. Both agencies prefer that you send your complaint in writing. And it's very likely that you will be complaining about home furnishings, auto repairs, and home improvement problems, for those head the list in this state. The addresses and phone numbers of these agencies are listed below.

Administrator
Department of Consumer Affairs
Jim Thorpe Bldg., Room 460
Oklahoma City, Oklahoma 73105
(405) 521-3653

Assistant Attorney General
  for Consumer Protection
Office of Attorney General
State Capitol Bldg., Room 112
Oklahoma City, Oklahoma 73105
(405) 521-3921

OREGON

The success rate for the state agency in Oregon is better than sixty-three percent. They also publish a booklet that will tell you where to go for help with a specialized complaint called, straightforwardly enough, <u>Where To Go For a Specific Complaint</u>. If you are a resident of the state of Oregon, a copy is yours free for the asking from the Consumer Services Division. The agency will provide, on request, the latest consumer-oriented news from both federal and state sources. It will also act as a mediator between you and a business about which you have a complaint. Topping the list of complaints for Oregon consumers are misleading advertising, gasoline sales, and auto sales and repairs. Oregon has quite a few different places to contact with your complaints, some of them handling specific areas, which are noted in the listing below.

Chief Counsel
Consumer Protection Division
Office of Attorney General
1133 S.W. Market St.
Portland, Oregon 97201
(503) 229-5522

Administrator
Consumer Services Division
Department of Commerce
Salem, Oregon 97310
(503) 378-4320

Public Service Supervisor
Insurance Division
Commerce Department
158 12th St., N.E.
Salem, Oregon 97310
(503) 378-4271 (insurance only)

Information Director
Consumer Information
Public Utility Commission
Public Service Bldg.
Salem, Oregon 97310
(503) 378-6600 (utilities only)

Consumer Officer
Department of Agriculture
Agriculture Bldg., Room 201
635 Capitol St., N.E.
Salem, Oregon 97310
(503) 378-8298 (food, sanitation, short weight, agriculture products only)

PENNSYLVANIA

This state has some very helpful services for its consumers. For instance, the complaint form used by the state is available in Spanish as well as English. Or, if you have a complaint, and it's after 5:00 P.M., you can call your closest branch office and your call will be put through at no extra charge directly to the main office at Harrisburg, which remains open until 9:00 P.M. Those who are recipients of public assistance checks receive, along in their check envelope, a card full of consumer tips. The Bureau of Consumer Protection's success rate is well over sixty percent. Auto and home repairs, and problems with record and tapes are major sources for complaint.

For the addresses of the main and branch offices, see below.

Deputy Attorney General and Director
Bureau of Consumer Protection
Office of Attorney General
301 Market St.
Harrisburg, Pennsylvania 17101
(717) 787-9714

Branch Offices
Bureau of Consumer Protection
Department of Justice
133 N. Fifth St.
Allentown, Pennsylvania 18102
(215) 821-0901

Special Assistant Attorney General
Department of Justice
919 State St.
Erie, Pennsylvania 16501
(814) 454-7184

Deputy Attorney General
Harrisburg Regional Office
Bureau of Consumer Protection
Department of Justice
25 S. 3rd St.
Harrisburg, Pennsylvania 17101
(717) 787-7109

Deputy Attorney General
Bureau of Consumer Protection
Department of Justice
300 Liberty Ave.
Pittsburgh, Pennsylvania 15222
(412) 565-5135

Deputy Attorney General
Bureau of Consumer Protection
Department of Justice
1835 Centre Ave.
Pittsburgh, Pennsylvania 15219
(412) 566-1500, Ext. 319

Deputy Attorney General
Bureau of Consumer Protection
Department of Justice
402 Connell Bldg.
129 N. Washington Ave.
Scranton, Pennsylvania 18503
(717) 961-4582

Director
Policy Holders Service and Protection
Department of Insurance
Finance Bldg., Room 408
Harrisburg, Pennsylvania 17120
(717) 787-1131 (insurance only)

Branch Offices
Regional Manager
Erie Regional Office
P.O. Box 6142
Erie, Pennsylvania 16512
(814) 454-2818

Regional Manager
Philadelphia Regional Office
1400 Spring Garden St.
Philadelphia, Pennsylvania 19130
(215) 238-7240

Regional Manager
Pittsburgh Regional Office
300 Liberty Ave.
State Office Bldg.
Pittsburgh, Pennsylvania 15222
(412) 565-5020

Consumer Affairs Coordinator
Department of Banking
P.O. Box 2155
Harrisburg, Pennsylvania 17120
(717) 787-1854 (consumer credit companies, state savings & loans, state banks)

Division of Consumer Affairs
Department of Agriculture
2301 N. Cameron St.
Harrisburg, Pennsylvania 17120
(717) 787-4737

RHODE ISLAND

The average time it takes to process a complaint in Rhode Island is about a week. When you combine that with a success rate of just ninety percent, it adds up to a very efficient state consumer protection agency. As with so many other states, automobile repairs and sales are the subject of most consumer's complaints. Home improvements and repairs and problems with swimming pools are also major areas for complaint. It's a good thing that every town in the state is within fifty miles of the state capital, Providence, because the two state consumer agencies have no branch offices. Here are the addresses and phone numbers of those agencies.

Executive Director
Rhode Island Consumers' Council
365 Broadway
Providence, Rhode Island 02902
(401) 277-2764

Administrator
Division of Consumer Protection
Department of Attorney General
56 Pine St.
Providence, Rhode Island 02903
(401) 277-3163

SOUTH CAROLINA

A welcome convenience for consumers in South Carolina is the Department of Consumer Affairs toll-free line, 800-922-1594. Consumers are urged to use it whenever they need to. The success rate of this comparatively new (established 1974) state agency is better than fifty percent. The average time needed to process a complaint is about a week. Finance and loan companies, auto repairs, mobile homes and mail-order houses are among the major problem areas.

Coordinator
Office of Citizens Service
Governor's Office

State House, P.O. Box 11450
Columbia, South Carolina 29211
(803) 758-3261

Administrator
Department of Consumer Affairs
Columbia Bldg., 6th Floor
1200 Main, P.O. Box 11739
Columbia, South Carolina 29211
(803) 758-2040

Assistant Attorney General for
  Consumer Protection
Office of Attorney General
Hampton Office Bldg.
P.O. Box 11549
Columbia, South Carolina 29211
(803) 758-3970

Division Director
Market Conduct Division
Department of Insurance
2711 Middleburg Dr.
P.O. Box 4067
Columbia, South Carolina 29204
(803) 758-2876 (insurance only)

SOUTH DAKOTA

Although there were no figures available for the success rate of this state's consumer agency, they do try to answer complaints within twenty-four hours. They prefer that the consumer write rather than call in the problem. The top problem areas in this state are mobile homes, mail-order houses, and retail stores. The address of the main office and its branch office are as follows:

Secretary
Department of Commerce and Consumer
  Affairs
State Capitol
Pierre, South Dakota 57401
(605) 224-3177

Investigator
Department of Commerce and Consumer Affairs
Division of Consumer Protection
Courthouse Plaza, Suite 2
Sioux Falls, South Dakota 27102
(605) 339-6691

TENNESSEE

Tennessee does not have much in the way of consumer protection legislation, and perhaps as a result, the success rate for their state consumer agency is only about twenty percent. Generally, it takes three or four weeks for action to be taken on a complaint. The subject of most complaints is vacation give-aways, followed by mail-order houses and home repairs. One bright spot is the Department of Agriculture's toll-free number for complaints; 800-342-8385.

Director
Division of Consumer Affairs
Department of Agriculture
Lab and Office Bldg.
Ellington Agricultural Center
Hogan Rd., Box 40627
Melrose Station
Nashville, Tennessee 37204
(615) 741-1461

Assistant Attorney General
　for Consumer Protection
Office of Attorney General
Supreme Court Bldg.,
Room 415
Nashville, Tennessee 37219
(615) 471-1671

TEXAS

The great state of Texas has a great success rate for their state agency. Seventy-five percent of their cases are resolved successfully. This is another state that has two statewide agencies. The Antitrust and Consumer Protection Division of the Attorney General's Office has broad legal powers to help the consumer. The other agency does not have such strong power, but it can act as a mediator in consumer/business disputes. Perhaps because of the great volume of complaints they receive, about 10,000 a year, the waiting time for processing a complaint is about four weeks. The consumer problems that plague the rest of the nation also bother Texans. That's right, auto repairs and sales, mobile homes, and home improvement troubles are the source of many complaints here. Landlord-tenant relations are another source of contention. Luckily, these agencies have branch offices scattered throughout the state for your convenience. Here are the addresses where you can reach them.

Assistant Attorney General and Chief
Consumer Protection Division
Office of Attorney General
P.O. Box 12548

Capitol Station
Austin, Texas 78711
(512) 682-4547

Branch Offices
Assistant Attorney General
4313 N. 10th
McAllen, Texas 78501
(512) 682-4547

Assistant Attorney General
North Texas Regional Office
2930 Turtle Creek Plaza
Dallas, Texas 75219
(214) 742-8944

Assistant Attorney General
City-County Bldg.
El Paso, Texas 79901
(915) 533-3484

Assistant Attorney General
County Office Bldg.
806 Broadway
Lubbock, Texas 79401
(806) 747-5238

Assistant Attorney General
100 Dwyer Ave.
San Antonio, Texas 78204
(512) 224-1007

Assistant Attorney General
369 One Main Plaza
Houston, Texas 77002
(713) 228-0701

Consumer Center
201 E. Belknap St.
Fort Worth, Texas 76102
(817) 334-1788

Commissioner
Office of Consumer Credit
1011 San Jacinto Blvd.
P.O. Box 2107
Austin, Texas 78767
(512) 475-2111 (consumer credit only)

Director
Consumer Affairs Office
Department of Agriculture
113 San Jacinto
Austin, Texas 78701
(512) 475-2154

Director
State Board of Insurance
State Insurance Bldg.
1110 San Jacinto Blvd.
Austin, Texas 78786
          (insurance only)
(512) 475-3726

UTAH

There are two areas that give problems to the residents of Utah that do not trouble the rest of the nation to any great degree. At the top of the list for consumer complaints are problems concerning the purchase of silver, and pyramid plans, where those who sign up first make money but everyone else after that loses money. After these two, consumers complain most about real estate and land development schemes and health spas. Your chances of the state agency resolving your complaint satisfactorily are better than half, and you can expect to wait about three weeks to get action of your problem.

If you should have a problem that has anything to do with credit, Utah does have an agency that deals specifically with problems of this kind. The address and phone number is included with the rest below.

Assistant Attorney General
Consumer Protection Division
Office of Attorney General
236 State Capitol
Salt Lake City, Utah 84114
(801) 533-6261

Administrator
Uniform Consumer Credit Code
Department of Financial Institutions
10 W. Broadway, Suite 331
Salt Lake City, Utah 84101
(801) 533-5461 (consumer credit only)

Director
Division of Consumer Affairs
Utah Trade Commission
Department of Business Regulation
330 E. Fourth St., South
Salt Lake City, Utah 84111
(801) 533-6441

VERMONT

Vermont's state agency has a success rate of better than sixty-five percent, and the waiting time to get action on your complaint is only about a week. This state also has an agency that specifically handles all problems that have to do with insurance. Major areas of concern to consumers here are mail-order houses, with the largest number of complaints, followed by home improvements or repairs and automobile repairs.

Commissioner
Department of Banking and Insurance
State Office Bldg., 120 State St.
Montpelier, Vermont 05602
(802) 828-3301 (insurance only)

Chief
Consumer Affairs Division
Vermont Public Service Board
120 State St.
Montpelier, Vermont 05602
(802) 828-2332

Assistant Attorney General in Charge
Consumer Fraud Division
Office of Attorney General
200 Main St., P.O. Box 981
Burlington, Vermont 05401
(802) 862-6730
(802) 658-4353

VIRGINIA

Most of the complaints that the Office of Consumer Affairs receives concern retail stores, mail-order houses, auto repairs and sales, and home repairs. Their success rate is over fifty percent, which is not bad. This agency usually advises consumers to get in touch with both the merchant and the manufacturer involved in the complaint before asking them to handle it. When you have exhausted all other avenues, they prefer you to send your complaint in writing, rather than call. To simplify matters they have a standard form for complaints, which you can request be sent to you. Also, if you feel you have not been treated in the best of ways by one of Virginia's state agencies, you can complain about it to the Office of Consumer Affairs by calling 800-552-9963 toll-free. Another handy consumer resource put out by the same agency is a series of pamphlets called There Is A Law in Virginia. They are available on request and contain valuable information on your rights as a consumer. All in all, Virginia seems to be making a worthy effort in protecting the consumers who reside within its boundaries. Check below for information about where you can contact these agencies or their branch offices.

Assistant Attorney General
Division of Consumer Counsel
Office of Attorney General
Supreme Court Bldg.
825 E. Broad St.
Richmond, Virginia 23219
(804) 786-2042

Administrator of Consumer Affairs
Office of Consumer Affairs
Department of Agriculture and Commerce
825 E. Broad St.
Richmond, Virginia 23219
(804) 786-2042
(800) 552-9963 (regarding state agencies)

Branch Office
8301 Arlington Blvd.
Fairfax, Virginia 22030
(703) 573-1286

Assistant Insurance Commissioner
Consumer Services and Marketing
Department of Insurance
Blanton Bldg., 6th Floor
Governor and Banks Sts.
P.O. Box 1157
Richmond, Virginia 23209
(804) 770-7691 (insurance only)

WASHINGTON

There's good news for the residents of Washington. It's the toll-free 'hot line' of the Consumer Protection and Antitrust Division. This seems to indicate a willingness on the part of this agency to take consumer complaints by phone, so be sure to take advantage of this service. Another fine service of this agency is its handy little book, <u>Consumer's Dozen Educator's Handbook</u>. This book gives details of laws regarding consumers' rights, and how to make those laws work for you. Though there are no figures for rate of success or waiting time, judging from the services it provides it is a pretty good bet that this is an efficiently run agency. Check below for that toll-free number and for the address of the office nearest you. And, by the way, if you're writing or calling with a complaint about mail-order houses, retail stores, or auto repairs, you'll feel right at home, for these categories are major concerns for a lot of other consumers in Washington.

Senior Assistant Attorney General
  and Chief
Consumer Protection and Antitrust
  Division
Office of Attorney General
1266 Dexter Horton Bldg.
710 Second Ave.
Seattle, Washington 98104
(206) 464-7744
(800) 552-0700 (toll-free)

Senior Assistant Attorney General and Chief
Spokane Office of Attorney General
1305 Old National Bank Bldg.
Spokane, Washington 99201
(509) 456-3123

Senior Consumer Specialist
Office of Consumer Services
Department of Agriculture
406 General Administration Bldg.
Olympia, Washington 98504
(206) 753-0029 (food, agricultural products, poison prevention only)

WEST VIRGINIA

The success rate in this state is well over eighty percent, and, with some exceptions, the average waiting time for action is about four weeks. The exceptions are those complaints concerning mobile homes and automobiles, which usually take a good deal longer to process. One especially welcome service are the Consumer Protection Divisions within various departments that deal specifically with certain kinds of consumer complaints. The CPD of the Department of Agriculture handles problems that concern agricultural products and food. The Department of Labor's CPD works with mobile home safety complaints, weights and measures, and problems concerning the safety of bedding and upholstery. Their addresses are included in the listings below. As might be expected from the above information, the top three complaint areas in this state are mobile homes, auto repairs and sales, and home improvements.

Director
Consumer Protection Division
Office of Attorney General
State Capitol Bldg.
Charleston, West Virginia 25305
(304) 348-8986

Director
Consumer Protection Division
Department of Agriculture
State Capitol, Room E-111
Charleston, West Virginia 25305
(305) 348-2226

Director
Consumer Protection Division
Department of Labor
1900 Washington St., E.
Charleston, West Virginia 25305
(304) 348-7890

WISCONSIN

If you submit a complaint to this state's Office of Consumer Protection, you will receive an acknowledgment of that complaint within three days. Action begins on the complaint within two weeks, but a successful resolution may take as long as six weeks. Still, it may be worth the wait, because this agency's success rate is about sixty percent. Used cars, home repairs and automobile sales are what consumers are complaining about the most in Wisconsin, which puts them in line with much of the rest of the country. If you have a complaint, your chances are good for some personal treatment, for the state agencies here have quite a few branch offices.

Chairman
Governor's Council for Consumer
  Affairs
V29E Capitol
Madison, Wisconsin 53702
(608) 266-3104

Consumer Affairs Coordinator
Office of Consumer Protection
Wisconsin Department of Justice
State Capitol
Madison, Wisconsin 53702
(608) 266-7340

Assistant Attorney General
Office of Consumer Protection
Department of Justice
State Capitol
Madison, Wisconsin 53702
(608) 266-1852

Director
Bureau of Consumer Protection
Trade Division
Department of Agriculture
801 W. Badger Rd.
Madison, Wisconsin 53713
(608) 266-7228

WYOMING

For residents of this state, the state agencies are just about the only game in town. However, with a success rate of about seventy-five percent and a waiting time of only about three weeks, it is a game well worth playing. This agency can also act as mediator or arbitrator for the consumer on an informal basis. Most complaints concern appliances and appliance repairs, auto repairs, and mobile home parks. Here's where to write or phone with your problem.

Special Assistant Attorney General
Office of Attorney General
Capitol Bldg.
Cheyenne, Wyoming 82002
(307) 777-7384

State Examiner and Administrator
Consumer Credit Code
Supreme Court Bldg.
Cheyenne, Wyoming 82002
(307) 777-7797 (consumer credit
  only)

Chapter 5:
COMPLAINING TO THE MANUFACTURERS

An advertiser can seldom make money selling you something only once. Therefore, most major companies genuinely want to hear from you when you have a valid complaint. It not only helps them keep you as a customer, but when the complaint occurs often enough, it enables them to remedy some defect in the product.

It always helps to write directly to the president of the company by name. In this chapter we've listed major national advertisers with complete address and company president. Although the president of General Motors may not cancel his board meeting to answer your complaint, you stand an excellent chance of it being directed to the right person.

The name of most "parent" companies appears on the product so therefore it is necessary to look beyond the trademark brand name to know where to write. For example, if you have a problem with Maxwell House Coffee, you'll need to look on the can to see that it is a product of General Foods. This directory will then tell you whom to write to at General Foods.

Obviously this section can only list the major advertisers. In other cases you'll have to look for the manufacturer's name and address on the product. It is frankly worth it (on a major complaint) to call the company to find the name of the president; when your letter is addressed to him by name you stand a better chance of response than when you have simply addressed a letter to the man by title.

PRESIDENTS OF COMPANIES
ALPHABETICALLY LISTED
BY CATEGORY

ACCESSORIES, LUGGAGE, JEWELRY

AMITY LEATHER PRODUCTS CO.
South Main Street
West Bend, WI 53095
Robert T. Rolfs

MARK CROSS, INC.
645 Fifth Avenue
New York, NY 10022
Edward Wasserberger

DANTE'
(Subsidiary of Genesco, Inc.)
1290 Avenue of Americas
New York, NY 10019
Steve McMullen

HICKOK MFG. CO., INC.
P. O. Box 5963
Arlington, TX 76011
John C. Scheffel

KAYSER-ROTH CORPORATION
640 Fifth Avenue
New York, NY 10019
James I. Spiegel

KREISLER MFG. CORP.
2600 22nd Street North
St. Petersburg, FL 33710
Edward Stern

L'EGGS PRODUCTS INC.
(Division of Hanes Corp.)
P. O. Box 2495
Winston-Salem, NC 27102
Joe Neeley

ACCESSORIES, LUGGAGE, JEWELRY

MIGHTY-MAC
Emerson Avenue
Gloucester, MA 01930
Richard S. Bell

SAMSONITE CORPORATION
(Subsidiary of Beatrice Foods Co.)
11200 East 45th Avenue
Denver, CO 80239
Irving J. Shwayder

SWANK, INC.
90 Park Avenue
New York, NY 10016
Marshall Tulin

AUTOMOBILES & TRUCKS

AMERICAN MOTORS CORPORATION
American Center
2777 Franklin Road
Southfield, MI 48034
G. C. Meyers

CHRYSLER CORPORATION
P. O. Box 1919
Detroit, MI 48288
E. A. Cafiero

FIAT MOTORS OF NORTH AMERICA, INC.
(Subsidiary of Fiat, S.P.A., Torino, Italy)
155 Chestnut Ridge Road
Montvale, NJ 07645
C. Ferrari

AUTOMOBILES & TRUCKS

FORD MOTOR COMPANY
The American Road
Dearborn, MI 48121
Lee A. Iacocca

GENERAL MOTORS CORPORATION
General Motors Building
Detroit, MI 48202
Elliott M. Estes

INTERNATIONAL HARVESTER COMPANY
401 North Michigan Avenue
Chicago, IL 60611
Archie R. McCardell

MACK TRUCKS, INC.
Mack Boulevard, Box M
Allentown, PA 18105
Alfred W. Pelletier

RYDER TRUCK LINES, INC.
(Subsidiary of IU International)
2050 Kings Road
Jacksonville, FL 32203
E. N. Hoekenga

TOYOTA MOTOR SALES, U.S.A., INC.
(Subsidiary of Toyota Motor Sales
  Co., Ltd.)
2055 West 190th St., P.O. Box 2991
Torrance, CA 90509
I. Makino

VOLKSWAGEN OF AMERICA, INC.
(Subsidiary of Volkswagenwerk AG)
818 Sylvan Avenue
Englewood Cliffs, NJ 07632
J. Stuart Perkins

CLEANING AGENTS

BOYLE-MIDWAY
(Division of American Home
  Products Corporation)
685 Third Avenue
New York, NY 10017
J. W. Culligan

CLEANING AGENTS

CALGON CORPORATION
(Subsidiary of Merck & Co., Inc.)
Calgon Center
Pittsburgh, PA 15230
A. L. Goeschel

THE CLOROX COMPANY
1221 Broadway
Oakland, CA 94612
R. B. Shetterly

THE DRACKETT CO.
(Subsidiary of Bristol-Myers Co.)
5020 Spring Grove Avenue
Cincinnati, OH 45232
N. M. Evans

S. C. JOHNSON & SON, INC.
1525 Howe
Racine, WI 53403
W. K. Eastham

THE KIWI POLISH COMPANY (U.S.A.)
2 High Street
Pottstown, PA 19464
Michael A. Burnett

LEVER BROTHERS COMPANY
390 Park Avenue
New York, NY 10022
Thomas S. Carroll

THE PROCTER & GAMBLE CO.
P. O. Box 599
Cincinnati, OH 45201
J. G. Smale

PUREX CORPORATION
5101 Clark Avenue
Lakewood, CA 90712
W. R. Tincher

UNITED STATES BORAX & CHEMICAL
  CORP.
3075 Wilshire Blvd., P.O. Box 75128
Los Angeles, CA 90010
Dr. Carl Randolph

FOOD PRODUCTS

A & W INTERNATIONAL, INC.
(Subsidiary of United Brands Co.)
922 Broadway
Santa Monica, CA 90406
James C. Doherty

AMERICAN BEVERAGE CORP.
117th & 15th Avenue
College Point, NY 11356
Samuel Baker

AMERICAN HOME FOODS
(Division of American Home Products Corp.)
685 Third Avenue
New York, NY 10017
D. P. Jaicks

AMERICAN KITCHEN PRODUCTS CO.
(Affiliate of S. Gumpert Co., Inc.)
812 Jersey Avenue
Jersey City, NJ 07302
R. G. Janover

AMERICAN MAIZE PRODUCTS COMPANY
250 Park Avenue
New York, NY 10017
P. E. Ramstad

AMERICAN POP CORN CO.
Sioux City, IA 51102
Wrede Smith

AMSTAR CORPORATION
1251 Avenue of the Americas
New York, NY 10020
Robert T. Quittmeyer

ANDERSON CLAYTON FOODS
(Division of Anderson, Clayton & Co.)
P.O. Box 6165, 7839 Churchill Way
Dallas, TX 75222
Robert McDonald

ANHEUSER-BUSCH, INC.
721 Pestalozzi
St. Louis, MO 63118
August A. Busch, III

FOOD PRODUCTS

ARM & HAMMER DIV. OF CHURCH & DWIGHT CO., INC.
Two Pennsylvania Plaza
New York, NY 10001
Dwight C. Minton

ARMOUR AND COMPANY
(Subsidiary of Greyhound Corp.)
Greyhound Tower
Phoenix, AZ 85077
Albert S. Drain

ARNOLD BAKERS, INC.
10 Hamilton Avenue
Greenwich, CT 06830
Robert P. Kirby

AUNT NELLIE'S FOODS, INC.
(Subsidiary of Beatrice Foods Co.)
Clyman, WI 53016
David C. Lau

BACHMAN FOODS, INC., A CO. OF CULBRO CORP.
605 Third Avenue
New York, NY 10016
Don R. Brunett

BANQUET FOODS CORPORATION
(Subsidiary of RCA Corp.)
100 North Broadway
St. Louis, MO 63102
F. F. Smiley

BARTON'S CANDY CORPORATION
80 DeKalb Avenue
Brooklyn, NY 11201
George Klein

BASKIN ROBBINS 31 FLAVORS
(Subsidiary of J. Lyons & Co. Ltd., London, England)
1201 South Victory Boulevard
Burbank, CA 91506
Robert J. Hudecek

BEATRICE FOODS CO.
120 South LaSalle
Chicago, IL 60603
Wallace N. Rasmussen

FOOD PRODUCTS

BEECH-NUT FOODS CORPORATION
(Formerly Baker/Beech-Nut Corp.)
P. O. Box 127
Fort Washington, PA 19034
F. C. Nicholas

BOOTH FISHERIES
(Division of Consolidated Foods
 Corp.)
2 North Riverside Plaza
Chicago, IL 60606
Frank W. Holas

BORDEN, INC.
277 Park Avenue
New York, NY 10017
Eugene J. Sullivan

BORDEN INC. CRACKER JACK DIV.
4800 West 66th
Chicago, IL 60638
N. J. Dunkirk

BROCK CANDY COMPANY
4120 Jersey Pike
Chattanooga, TN 37421
P. K. Brock

BUITONI FOODS CORPORATION
450 Huyler Street
South Hackensack, NJ 07606
Marco Buitoni

BUMBLE BEE SEAFOODS
(Division of Castle & Cooke, Inc.)
50 California Street
San Francisco, CA 94111
John S. McGowan

CPC INTERNATIONAL
International Plaza
Englewood Cliffs, NJ 07632
James W. McKee, Jr.

CAMPBELL SOUP COMPANY
Camden, NJ 08101
H. A. Shaub

FOOD PRODUCTS

CANADA DRY CORPORATION
(Subsidiary of Norton Simon, Inc.)
100 Park Avenue
New York, NY 10017
Richard C. Beeson

CARNATION CO.
5045 Wilshire Boulevard
Los Angeles, CA 90036
D. L. Stuart

CARVEL CORPORATION
201 Saw Mill River Road
Yonkers, NY 10701
Thomas Carvel

CHARMS CO.
Halls Mill Road
Freehold, NJ 07728
V. Ciccone

CHIQUITA BRANDS INC.
(Subsidiary of United Brands, Inc.)
95 Chestnut Ridge Road
Montvale, NJ 07645
Anthony Depama

CHOCK FULL O'NUTS CORP.
425 Lexington Avenue
New York, NY 10017
Sy Mindel

CLAUSSEN PICKLE COMPANY, INC.
(Subsidiary of Oscar Mayer & Co.)
1300 Dane Street
Woodstock, IL 60098
Terry Flanagan

COCA-COLA USA
(Division of The Coca-Cola Co.)
310 North Avenue N.W.
Atlanta, GA 30318
John Ogden

CONSOLIDATED FOODS CORPORATION
135 South LaSalle
Chicago, IL 60603
John J. Cardwell

FOOD PRODUCTS

COTT CORPORATION
197 Chatham
New Haven, CT 06513
Carl Glickman

COUNTRY PRIDE FOODS LTD.
(Formerly J. M. Poultry Packing
  Co., Ltd.)
422 North Washington
El Dorado, AR 71730
R. C. Merkle

PATRICK CUDAHY INCORPORATED
Cudahy, WI 53110
A. T. Anderson

DAD'S ROOT BEER COMPANY
(An I. C. Industries Co.)
2800 North Talman Avenue
Chicago, IL 60618
Jules Klapman

DAIRYLEA COOPERATIVE INC.
1 Blue Hill Plaza
Pearl River, NY 10965
Richard E. Redmond

DANNON MILK PRODUCTS
(Subsidiary of Beatrice Foods Co.)
22-11 38th Avenue
Long Island City, NY 11101
Joseph Kagan

DEL MONTE CORP.
P. O. Box 3575
San Francisco, CA 94119
R. G. Landis

DIAMOND CRYSTAL SALT CO.
916 South Riverside
St. Clair, MI 48079
C. D. Cronenworth

DR. PEPPER COMPANY
Box 5086
Dallas, TX 75222
W. W. Clements

FOOD PRODUCTS

DOXSEE FOOD CORPORATION
8323 Pulaski Highway
Baltimore, MD 21237
Joseph Appelbaum

DUFFY-MOTT CO., INC.
370 Lexington Avenue
New York, NY 10017
R. M. Anrig

DUNKIN' DONUTS OF AMERICA, INC.
(Division of Dunkin' Donuts, Inc.)
P. O. Box 317
Randolph, MA 02368
Robert Rosenberg

DURKEE FOODS DIVISION OF SCM
 CORP., CONSUMER FOODS GROUP
900 Union Commerce Building
Cleveland, OH 44115
R. E. Dorfmeyer

THE R. T. FRENCH COMPANY
1 Mustard Street
Rochester, NY 14609
E. I. Reveal

FRITO-LAY, INC.
Frito-Lay Tower
Dallas, TX 75235
Wayne Calloway

GENERAL FOODS CORPORATION
250 North Street
White Plains, NY 10625
R. Barzelay

GENERAL MILLS, INC.
9200 Wayzata Boulevard
Minneapolis, MN 55440
H. B. Atwater, Jr.

GERBER PRODUCTS CO.
445 State Street
Fremont, MI 49412
Arthur J. Frens

FOOD PRODUCTS

THE GORTON GROUP
(Division of General Mills, Inc.)
327 Main
Gloucester, MA 01930
Ross Clouston

GOYA FOODS, INC.
100 Seaview Drive
Secaucus, NJ 07094
Joseph Unanue

THE GREAT ATLANTIC & PACIFIC TEA
  COMPANY, INC.
Two Paragon Drive
Montvale, NJ 07645
G. C. Gentry

GREEN GIANT CO.
Hazeltine Gates Office Park
Chaska, MN 55318
Thomas H. Wyman

HAWTHORN MELLODY, INC.
(Subsidiary of National Industries, Inc.)
4201 West Chicago Avenue
Chicago, IL 60651
J. E. Spielman, Jr.

L. S. HEATH & SONS INC.
Robinson, IL 62454
John L. Heath

HEBREW NATIONAL KOSHER FOODS, INC.
58-80 Maurice Avenue
Maspeth, NY 11378
I. Pines

H. J. HEINZ COMPANY
1062 Progress
Pittsburgh, PA 15212
A. J. F. O'Reilly

HERSHEY FOODS CORP.
19 East Chocolate Avenue
Hershey, PA 17033
R. A. Zimmerman

FOOD PRODUCTS

HEUBLEIN INC. GROCERY PRODUCTS DIV.
1500 East Third Street
Oxnard, CA 93030
Hicks Waldron

HILLS BROS. COFFEE, INC.
2 Harrison
San Francisco, CA 94119
Paul J. Miller

GEO. A. HORMEL & CO.
Austin, MN 55912
I. J. Holton

HUNT-WESSON FOODS, INC.
(Subsidiary of Norton Simon, Inc.)
1645 West Valencia Drive
Fullerton, CA 92634
William Hood

ITT CONTINENTAL BAKING CO., INC.
P. O. Box 731
Halstead Ave., Rye, NY 10580
M. C. Woodward, Jr.

INTERNATIONAL MULTIFOODS CORP.
1200 Multifoods Building
Minneapolis, MN 55402
Darrell M. Runke

IROQUOIS BRANDS, LTD.
41 West Putnam
Greenwich, CT 06830
T. J. Fox

JAYS FOODS INC.
825 East 99th
Chicago, IL 60628
Leonard Japp, Sr.

KAUKAUNA KLUB CHEESES
(Division of International Multifoods Corp.)
Kaukauna, WI 54130
G. A. Youso

KEEBLER COMPANY
One Hollow Tree Lane
Elmhurst, IL 60126
T. T. Garvin

FOOD PRODUCTS

KELLOGG COMPANY
Battle Creek, MI 49016
W. E. LaMothe

KITCHENS OF SARA LEE
(Division of Consolidated Foods
 Corp.)
500 Waukegan Road
Deerfield, IL 60015
Thomas F. Barnum

KRAFT, INC.
Kraft Court
Glenview, IL 60025
A. W. Woelfle

LA CHOY FOOD PRODUCTS DIVISION
 BEATRICE FOODS CO.
Stryker Street
Archbold, OH 43502
J. J. McRobbie

LAND O'LAKES INC.
614 McKinley Place
Minneapolis, MN 55413
Ralph Hofstad

LAWRY'S FOODS, INC.
568 San Fernando Road
Los Angeles, CA 90065
Richard N. Frank

LEA & PERRINS, INC.
Pollitt Drive
Fair Lawn, NJ 07410
James F. Lunn

LIBBY, MC NEILL & LIBBY
200 South Michigan Avenue
Chicago, IL 60604
D. B. Wells

LIFE SAVERS INC.
(Subsidiary of Squibb Corp.)
40 West 57th Street
New York, NY 10019
William M. Morris

FOOD PRODUCTS

THOMAS J. LIPTON, INC.
800 Sylvan Avenue
Englewood Cliffs, NJ 07632
H. M. Tibbetts

LOUIS SHERRY, INC.
18 West Putnam Avenue
Greenwich, CT 06830
Joseph P. Anniello

LUDEN'S INCORPORATED
200 North Eighth
Reading, PA 19603
P. F. Norton

THE B. MANISCHEWITZ CO.
340 Henderson Street
Jersey City, NJ 07302
Robert M. Starr

MARS, INCORPORATED
1651 Old Meadow Rd., Westgate Park
McLean, VA 22101
H. G. Klotz

MC CORMICK & CO., INC., GROCERY
 PRODUCTS DIVISION
McCormick Building
Baltimore, MD 21202
H. K. Wells

MELITTA INC.
(Subsidiary of Melitta-Werke Bentz
 & Sohn, Minden, Germany)
1401 Berlin Road
Cherry Hill, NJ 08003
Werner von Pein, Jr.

MILLER BREWING COMPANY
(An Operating Co. of Philip Mor-
 ris, Inc.)
3939 West Highland Boulevard
Milwaukee, WI 53201
John A. Murphy

JOHN MORRELL & CO.
(Subsidiary of United Brands Co.)
208 South LaSalle Street
Chicago, IL 60604
William Conroy

FOOD PRODUCTS

MORTON FOODS, INC.
6333 Denton Drive
Dallas, TX 75235
Sam Phillips

MORTON SALT
(Division of Morton-Norwich Products, Inc.)
110 North Wacker Drive
Chicago, Il 60606
Daniel A. Gescheidle

MRS. PAUL'S KITCHENS, INC.
5830 Henry Avenue
Philadelphia, PA 19128
E. J. Piszek

MRS. SMITH'S PIE CO.
South & Charlotte Streets
Pottstown, PA 19464
David L. Stevenson

C. F. MUELLER COMPANY
180 Baldwin Avenue
Jersey City, NJ 07306
Lester R. Thurston, Jr.

NABISCO, INC.
East Hanover, NJ 07936
Val B. Diehl

NATIONAL TEA CO.
9701 West Higgins Road
Rosemont, IL 60018
V. Schulz

THE NESTLE COMPANY, INC.
100 Bloomingdale Road
White Plains, NY 10605
David E. Guerrant

OCEAN SPRAY CRANBERRIES INC.
Plymouth, MA 02360
Harold Thorkilsen

ORE-IDA FOODS, INC.
(Subsidiary of H. J. Heinz Co.)
Boise, ID 83707
Paul I. Cordry

FOOD PRODUCTS

OSCAR MAYER & CO.
910 Mayer Ave., P.O.Box 7188
Madison, WI 53707
Jerry M. Hiegel

OVALTINE PRODUCTS INC.
1 Ovaltine Court
Villa Park, IL 60181
Pierre Lansel

PABST BREWING COMPANY
917 West Juneau Avenue
Milwaukee, WI 53201
Frank C. DeGuire

PARKS SAUSAGE CO.
501 West Hamburg Street
Baltimore, MD 21230
R. V. Haysbert, Sr.

PETER PAUL, INC.
New Haven Road
Naugatuck, CT 06770
L. W. Elston

PEPPERIDGE FARM INC.
(Subsidiary of Campbell Soup Co.)
Westport Avenue
Norwalk, CT 06856
R. G. McGovern

PEPSI-COLA COMPANY
(Division of PepsiCo, Inc.)
Pepsico World Headquarters
Purchase, NY 10577
John Sculley

PERDUE INC.
P. O. Box 1537
Salisbury, MD 21801
Franklin P. Perdue

PET INCORPORATED
400 South Fourth Street
St. Louis, MO 63166
Boyd F. Schenk

PETER PAN SEAFOODS, INC.
1220 Dexter Horton Building
Seattle, WA 98104
Jay S. Gage

FOOD PRODUCTS

PFAELZER BROTHERS
(Division of Armour & Co.)
4501 West District Boulevard
Chicago, IL 60632
Candido Marquez

PFEIFFER'S FOODS
(Division of Hunt-Wesson)
5820 Main Street
Buffalo, NY 14221
William J. Hoffman

S. S. PIERCE CO., INC.
(Formerly Seneca Foods Corp.)
74 Seneca Street
Dundee, NY 14837
Arthur Wolcott

PILLSBURY COMPANY
608 Second Avenue South
Minneapolis, MN 55402
Winston R. Wallin

PLUMROSE
65 Springfield Avenue
Springfield, NJ 07081
Knud Sorensen

POPSICLE INDUSTRIES
(Division of Consolidated Foods
 Corp.)
110 Route 4
Englewood, NJ 07631
John P. Polychron

PRESTO FOOD PRODUCTS, INC.
929 East 14th
Los Angeles, CA 90021
Melvin S. Morse

PRINCE MACARONI MFG. CO.
Prince Avenue
Lowell, MA 01853
Joseph P. Pellegrino

PROGRESSO FOODS CORP.
(Subsidiary of Imasco Foods Corp.)
365 West Passaic Street
Rochelle Park, NJ 07662
Gasper F. Taormina

FOOD PRODUCTS

THE QUAKER OATS CO.
Merchandise Mart Plaza
Chicago, IL 60654
Kenneth Mason

QUAKER OATS CO. BURRY DIV.
1265 Durant Street
Elizabeth, NJ 07207
A. R. Ryan

RAGU FOODS, INC.
(Packaged Foods Division of Chese-
 brough-Pond's Inc.)
33 Benedict Place
Greenwich, CT 06830
C. J. Chapman

RALSTON PURINA COMPANY
Checkerboard Square
St. Louis, MO 63188
W. M. Shapleigh

RED CHEEK, INC.
Fleetwood, PA 19522
B. Rickenback

REED CANDY CO.
(Subsidiary of H. P. Hood, Inc.)
One Crossroads of Commerce
Rolling Meadows, IL 60008
Lawrence L. Anderson

RONZONI MACARONI CO., INC.
50-02 Northern Boulevard
Long Island City, NY 11101
Emanuele Ronzoni, Jr.

ROYAL CROWN COLA CO., SOFT DRINK
 DIVISION
1000 Tenth Avenue, P.O.Box 1440
Columbus, GA 31902
James J. Harford

S & W FINE FOODS, INC.
1730 South El Camino Real
P.O.Box 5580, San Mateo, CA 94402
Norman L. Correla

FOOD PRODUCTS

SACRAMENTO FOODS DIVISION OF
 BORDEN FOODS, BORDEN INC.
P. O. Box 2470
Sacramento, CA 95811
W. Van Benthuysen

SALADA FOODS INC. -- U. S. DIVISION
(Subsidiary of Kellogg Co.)
235 Porter Street
Battle Creek, MI 49016
William E. LaMothe

SALERNO-MEGOWEN BISCUIT CO.
7777 North Caldwell Avenue
Niles, IL 60648
Charles L. Sullivan

SAU-SEA FOODS, INC.
Yonkers, NY 10702
Ernest J. Schoenbrun

JOS. SCHLITZ BREWING CO.
235 West Galena, P.O. Box 614
Milwaukee, WI 53201
F. J. Sellinger

S. A. SCHOENBRUNN & CO., INC.
(Subsidiary of American Maize
 Products Co.)
Twenty-One Grand Avenue
Palisades Park, NJ 07650
George M. Brunner

SCHWEPPES U.S.A. LTD.
1200 High Ridge Road
Stamford, CT 06905
John B. Onthank

SEABROOK FOODS, INC.
(A Springs Co.)
P. O. Box 306
Montezuma, GA 31063
Jerre L. Pearson

THE SEVEN-UP COMPANY
121 South Meramec
St. Louis, MO 63105
W. E. Winter

FOOD PRODUCTS

STANDARD BRANDS INC.
625 Madison Avenue
New York, NY 10022
Reuben Gutoff

STANDARD BRANDS CONFECTIONERY DIV.
3638 Broadway
Chicago, IL 60613
Ronald T. Cappadocia

STANDARD MILLING CO.
1009 Central
Kansas City, MO 64105
Paul Uhlmann, Jr.

STAR-KIST FOODS, INC.
(Subsidiary of H. J. Heinz Co.)
Terminal Island, CA 90731
J. G. Scharer

STELLA-D'ORO BISCUIT CO., INC.
184 West 237th
Bronx, NY 10463
F. Zambetti

STOKELY-VAN CAMP, INC.
941 North Meridian
Indianapolis, IN 46206
Alfred J. Stokely

SUNKIST GROWERS, INC.
14130 Riverside Drive
Sherman Oaks, CA 91423
Roy Utke

SUNSHINE BISCUITS, INC.
(Subsidiary of American Brands
 Inc.)
245 Park Avenue
New York, NY 10017
Edward J. Jennings

SWIFT & COMPANY
(Subsidiary of Esmark, Inc.)
115 West Jackson Boulevard
Chicago, IL 60604
Alistair Sym Smith

FOOD PRODUCTS

TETLEY INC.
522 Fifth Avenue
New York, NY 10036
Charles Arnett

TOOTSIE ROLL INDUSTRIES, INC.
7401 South Cicero Avenue
Chicago, IL 60629
M. J. Gordon

TOPPS CHEWING GUM, INC.
254 36th Street
Brooklyn, NY 11232
Joel J. Shorin

TROPICANA PRODUCTS, INC.
Bradenton, FL 33506
Kenneth A. Barnebey

UNCLE BEN'S FOODS
(Division of Mars Inc.)
P. O. Box 1752
Houston, TX 77001
John J. Coady

UNIVERSAL FOODS CORP.
433 East Michigan
Milwaukee, WI 53201
J. L. Murray

VAN CAMP SEA FOOD CO.
(Division of Ralston Purina Co.)
11555 Sorrento Valley Road
San Diego, CA 92121
Stephen A. Brennen

VIENNA SAUSAGE MFG. CO.
2501 North Damen
Chicago, IL 60647
William Ladany

VITA-PAKT CITRUS PRODUCTS CO.
707 North Barranca Street
Covina, CA 91722
Milton F. Fillius, Jr.

VLASIC FOODS INC.
14 Mile Road
West Bloomfield, MI 48033
Dennis Sullivan

FOOD PRODUCTS

WELCH FOOD INC.
(Owned by National Grape Cooperative Association)
Westfield, NY 14787
N. M. Brown

WILSON FOODS CORPORATION
(Subsidiary of LTV Corp.)
4545 North Lincoln Boulevard
Oklahoma City, OK 73105
K. J. Griggy

WISE FOODS/BORDEN, INC.
Berwick, PA 18603
Clayton C. Daley

WM. WRIGLEY JR. COMPANY
410 North Michigan Avenue
Chicago, IL 60611
William Wrigley

WYLER FOODS/BORDEN INC.
2301 Shermer Road
Northbrook, IL 60062
John J. Hettinger

GAMES, TOYS, HOBBIES

AURORA PRODUCTS CORP.
(Subsidiary of Nabisco, Inc.)
44 Cherry Valley Road
West Hempstead, NY 11552
Boyd Browne

CHEMTOY CORP.
4700 West 19th Street
Cicero, IL 60650
Jerome Kalish

COLECO INDUSTRIES INC.
945 Asylum Avenue
Hartford, CT 06103
Arnold Greenberg

COLORFORMS, INC.
Norwood, NJ 07648
Harry Kislevitz

GAMES, TOYS, HOBBIES

CREATIVE PLAYTHINGS
(Operating Co. of CBS Toys Div.)
Princeton, NJ 08540
Seymour L. Gartenberg

FISHER-PRICE TOYS DIV. OF QUAKER
   OATS CO.
636 Girard Avenue
East Aurora, NY 14052
H. H. Coords

FUNDIMENSIONS, DIV. OF GENERAL
   MILLS FUN GROUP, INC.
26750-23 Mile Road
Mt. Clemens, MI 48043
Jim Boosales

IDEAL TOY CORPORATION
200 Fifth Avenue North
New York, NY 10010
Lionel Weintraub

KENNER PRODUCTS DIV. OF GENERAL
   MILLS FUN GROUP, INC.
1014 Vine Street
Cincinnati, OH 45202
Bernie Loomis

KNICKERBOCKER TOY CO., INC.
(Division of Warner Communications,
   Inc.)
1107 Broadway
New York, NY 10010
Rod White

LEGO SYSTEMS, INC.
(Subsidiary of Lego Systems A/S)
555 Taylor Road
Enfield, CT 06082
John M. Sullivan

LEISURE DYNAMICS, INC.
4400 West 78th Street
Minneapolis, MN 55435
Louis F. Polk, Jr.

LOUIS MARX & CO., INC.
633 Hope Street
Stamford, CT 06904
Robert Butler

GAMES, TOYS, HOBBIES

MATTEL TOYS
(Division of Mattel, Inc.)
5150 Rosecrans Avenue
Hawthorne, CA 90250
Raymond P. Wagner

MEGO CORP.
(Subsidiary of Mego International,
   Inc.)
41 Madison Avenue
New York, NY 10010
Martin B. Abrams

MILTON BRADLEY CO.
1500 Main Street
East Longmeadow, MA 01028
James J. Shea, Jr.

THE OHIO ART CO.
Box 111, East High Street
Bryan, OH 43506
W. C. Killgallon

PARKER BROTHERS
(Subsidiary of General Mills,
   Inc.)
190 Bridge Street
Salem, MA 01970
Randolph P. Barton

PLAYSKOOL INC.
(Division of Milton Bradley Co.)
4501 West Augusta Boulevard
Chicago, IL 60651
Albert O. Laubinger

REVELL, INC.
4223 Glencoe Avenue
Venice (Los Angeles), CA 90291
Mrs. Royle Lasky

SCHAPER MANUFACTURING CO.
(Division of Kusan, Inc.)
9909 South Shore Drive
Minneapolis, MN 55441
W. L. Garrity

F. A. O. SCHWARZ
(Member of Franz Carl Weber Intl.)
745 Fifth Avenue
New York, NY 10022
Pieter Oechsle

GAMES, TOYS, HOBBIES

SELCHOW & RIGHTER CO.
2215 Union Boulevard
Bay Shore, NY 11706
F. A. Huettner

SOUTH BEND TOY MFG. CO.
(Subsidiary of Milton Bradley Co.)
P. O. Box 3675
South Bend, IN 46628
John T. Bycraft

TONKA CORP.
10505 Wayzata Boulevard
Hopkins, MN 55343
P. M. Wimsatt

TUDOR GAMES, INC.
176 Johnson
Brooklyn, NY 11201
Norman A. Sas

TYCO INDUSTRIES, INC.
(Division of Consolidated Foods)
540 Glen Avenue
Moorestown, NJ 08057
Richard E. Grey

UNEEDA DOLL COMPANY, INC.
200 Fifth Avenue
New York, NY 10010
Sam Sklarsky

THE UNITED STATES PLAYING CARD
  COMPANY
(Subsidiary of Diamond International Corp.)
Beech & Park
Cincinnati, OH 45212
A. C. Luther, Jr.

WHAM-O MANUFACTURING CO.
835 East El Monte
San Gabriel, CA 91778
James W. Kerrigan

GASOLINES & LUBRICANTS

AMERADA HESS CORP.
1185 Avenue of the Americas
New York, NY 10036
Philip Kramer

AMERICAN PETROFINA, INC.
(Subsidiary of American Petrofina
  Holding Co.)
P. O. Box 2159
Dallas, TX 75221
Paul D. Meek

AMOCO OIL COMPANY
(Subsidiary of Standard Oil Co. of
  Indiana)
200 East Randolph Street
Chicago, IL 60601
Walter R. Peirson

ASHLAND OIL, INC.
P. O. Box 391
Ashland, KY 41101
Norman R. Trimble

ATLANTIC RICHFIELD COMPANY
515 South Flower Street
Los Angeles, CA 90071
Thornton F. Bradshaw

B P OIL INC.
(Subsidiary of The Standard Oil
  Co. of Ohio)
Midland Building
Cleveland, OH 44115
J. D. Harnett

CENEX
1185 North Concord Street
South St. Paul, MN 55075
Jerry Tvedt

CHEKER OIL CO.
174th & Dixie Highway
East Hazelcrest, IL 60429
Richard P. Small

CHEVRON U.S.A. INC. NORTHEAST DIV.
1200 State Street
Perth Amboy, NJ 08861
H. D. Schmalzel

GASOLINES & LUBRICANTS

CITIES SERVICE COMPANY
P. O. Box 300
Tulsa, OK 74102
Charles J. Waidelich

CLARK OIL & REFINING CORP.
8530 West National Avenue
Milwaukee, WI 53227
G. W. Jandacek

CONOCO CHEMICALS DIV. OF CONTI-
 NENTAL OIL CO.
P.O. Box 2197, 5 Greenway Plaza
Houston, TX 77001
A. J. Lacazette

CONTINENTAL OIL COMPANY
High Ridge Park
Stamford, CT 06904
Howard W. Blauvelt

DIAMOND SHAMROCK CORP. - OIL &
 GAS UNIT
P. O. Box 631
Amarillo, TX 79173
Avery Rush, Jr.

ETHYL CORPORATION
330 South Fourth St., P.O. Box 2189
Richmond, VA 23217
Bruce C. Gottwald

EXXON CORPORATION
1251 Avenue of the Americas
New York, NY 10020
H. C. Kauffman

GETTY REFINING AND MARKETING COM-
 PANY
(Formerly: Skelly Oil Co.)
1437 South Boulder
Tulsa, OK 74102
J. D. Jones

GULF OIL CORPORATION
Gulf Building
Pittsburgh, PA 15230
James E. Lee

GASOLINES & LUBRICANTS

KERR-MC KEE CORPORATION
Kerr-McGee Center
Oklahoma City, OK 73125
D. A. McGee

KEWANEE INDUSTRIES, INC.
40 Morris Avenue, P.O. Box 591
Bryn Mawr, PA 19010
Andrew J. Bozzelli

MOBIL OIL CORP.
(Subsidiary of Mobil Corp.)
150 East 42nd Street
New York, NY 10017
W. P. Tavoulareas

PENNZOIL COMPANY
Pennzoil Place, 700 Milam
Houston, TX 77001
Baine P. Kerr

PHILLIPS PETROLEUM COMPANY
Bartlesville, OK 74004
William C. Douce

QUAKER STATE OIL REFINING CORPORA-
 TION
Quaker State Building
Oil City, PA 16301
Q. E. Wood

SHELL OIL COMPANY
P. O. Box 2463
Houston, TX 77001
J. F. Bookout

STANDARD OIL COMPANY (INDIANA)
(Parent Company Conducting Op-
 erations Through Subsidiaries)
200 East Randolph Drive
Chicago, IL 60601
George V. Myers

SUN COMPANY, INC.
100 Matsonford Road
Radnor, PA 19087
Theodore A. Burtis

GASOLINES & LUBRICANTS

TEXACO INC.
2000 Westchester Avenue
White Plains, NY 10650
John K. McKinley

UNION OIL CO. OF CALIFORNIA
461 South Boylston
Los Angeles, CA 90017
Fred L. Hartley

VICKERS PETROLEUM CORP.
(Subsidiary of Vickers Energy
 Corp.)
Vickers-KSB&T Building
Wichita, KS 67202
Harold Grueskin

HOUSE FURNISHINGS

AIRWICK INDUSTRIES, INC.
(Division of Ciba-Geigy Corp.)
380 North Street
Teterboro, NJ 07608
Frank W. Conkling

ANCHOR HOCKING CORP.
109 North Broad Street
Lancaster, OH 43130
George C. Barber

BALL CORPORATION
345 South High Street
Muncie, IN 47302
J. W. Fisher

BEACON MFG. CO.
104 West 40th Street
New York, NY 10018
Victor L. Fioravante

CANNON MILLS, INC.
1271 Avenue of the Americas
New York, NY 10020
Hugh J. Toumey

CORNING GLASS WORKS
Houghton Park
Corning, NY 14830
Thomas C. MacAvoy

HOUSE FURNISHINGS

CUISINARTS INC.
1 Barry Place
Stamford, CT 06902
Carl Sontheimer

THE d-CON CO., INC.
(Subsidiary of Sterling Drug Co.,
 Inc.)
90 Park Avenue
New York, NY 10016
Walter C. Camas

DUNDEE MILLS, INC.
P. O. Box 97
Griffin, GA 30223
J. M. Cheatham

EKCO HOUSEWARES CO.
(Division of American Home Prod-
 ucts Corp.)
9234 West Belmont Avenue
Franklin Park, IL 60131
J. K. Duncan

FARBERWARE SUB. OF WALTER KIDDE &
 COMPANY, INC.
1500 Bassett Avenue
Bronx, NY 10461
Arnold H. Dreyfuss

FIELDCREST DIV. OF FIELDCREST
 MILLS, INC.
60 West 40th Street
New York, NY 10018
David M. Tracy

FORT HOWARD PAPER CO.
1919 South Broadway
Green Bay, WI 54305
Paul J. Schierl

THE FULLER BRUSH CO.
(Subsidiary of Consolidated Foods
 Corp.)
P. O. Box 729
Great Bend, KS 67530
John J. Doumas

GRABER COMPANY
Graber Plaza
Middleton, WI 53562
Joseph S. Thiele

HOUSE FURNISHINGS

HOBART CORPORATION
World Headquarters
Troy, OH 45374
David B. Meeker

HUDSON PULP & PAPER CORP.
477 Madison Avenue
New York, NY 10022
D. Mazer

KRAZY GLUE INC.
(Division of B. Jadow & Sons)
4038 North Nashville Avenue
Chicago, IL 60634
B. Jadow

LENOX CHINA, INC.
Prince & Meade
Trenton, NJ 08605
H. H. Goucher

MOULINEX PRODUCTS INC.
(Subsidiary of Moulinex S.A.)
400 Cooper Center North
Pennsauken, NJ 08109
William G. Palese

ONEIDA LTD. SILVERSMITHS
Oneida, NY 13421
P. T. Noyes

OWENS-ILLINOIS INC., LILY DIV.
P. O. Box 1035
Toledo, OH 43666
C. D. "Doc" Pawlicki

REED & BARTON
144 West Britannia
Taunton, MA 02780
Sinclair Weeks, Jr.

REGAL WARE, INC.
Kewaskum, WI 53040
James D. Reigle

REVERE COPPER AND BRASS, INC.
605 Third Avenue
New York, NY 10016
W. F. Collins

HOUSE FURNISHINGS

RONSON CORP.
1 Ronson Road
Bridgewater, NJ 08807
Louis V. Aronson, II

RUBBERMAID INCORPORATED
Wooster, OH 44691
L. E. Gigax

SALTON, INC.
1260 Zerega Avenue
Bronx, NY 10462
James W. Lynch

SCOTT PAPER COMPANY
Scott Plaza
Philadelphia, PA 19113
C. D. Dickey, Jr.

SCOVILL MFG. CO., NUTONE DIV.
Madison & Red Bank Roads
Cincinnati, OH 45227
J. William Cahill

THE SOLO CUP CO.
1505 East Main Street
Urbana, IL 61801
L. J. Hulseman

SPRINGS MILLS, INC.
Fort Mill, SC 29715
Peter G. Scotese

STANLEY HOME PRODUCTS, INC.
333 Western Avenue
Westfield, MA 01085
Homer G. Perkins

TIFFANY & COMPANY
5th Avenue & 57th Street
New York, NY 10022
Henry B. Platt

WEDGWOOD, INC.
41 Madison Avenue
New York, NY 10010
Raymond Smyth

WEST POINT PEPPERELL
West 10th Street
West Point, GA 31833
Joseph L. Lanier, Jr.

HOUSEHOLD APPLIANCES

AMANA REFRIGERATION, INC.
Amana, IA 52204
George C. Foerstner

BISSELL INC.
Grand Rapids, MI 49501
J. M. Bissell

CALORIC CORPORATION
(Division of Raytheon Co.)
Topton, PA 19562
Kenneth J. Haas

ELECTROLUX
2777 Summer Street
Stamford, CT 06905
C. A. McKee

THE EUREKA COMPANY
(Division of National Union
 Electric Corp.)
Bloomington, IL 61701
H. W. Schaefer

GENERAL MOTORS CORP. FRIGIDAIRE
 DIVISION
300 Taylor
Dayton, OH 45442
Emmett B. Lewis

THE HOOVER CO.
101 East Maple Street
North Canton, OH 44720
F. L. Tabacchi

HOTPOINT (GENERAL ELECTRIC CO.)
Appliance Park
Louisville, KY 40225
J. R. Anderson

KELVINATOR APPLIANCE COMPANY
(Subsidiary of White Consolidated
 Industries, Inc.)
4248 Kalamazoo Street S.E.
Grand Rapids, MI 49508
C. C. Rieger

MAGIC CHEF, INC.
Cleveland, TN 37311
S. B. Rymer, Jr.

HOUSEHOLD APPLIANCES

THE MAYTAG COMPANY
Newton, IA 50208
Daniel J. Krumm

OSTER CORPORATION
(Subsidiary of Sunbeam Corp.)
5055 North Lydell
Milwaukee, WI 53217
L. S. Mattson

PROCTOR-SILEX
700 West Tabor Road
Philadelphia, PA 19120
H. Hill

THE REGINA COMPANY
(Unit of General Signal)
Regina Avenue
Rahway, NJ 07065
Earl Seitz

RIVAL MFG. CO.
36th at Bennington
Kansas City, MO 64129
John W. Breeden

ROPER SALES CORP.
(Division of Roper Corp.)
1905 West Court Street
Kankakee, IL 60901
John R. Keegan

SCHICK INCORPORATED
33 Riverside Avenue
Westport, CT 06880
James W. Hart

SUNBEAM APPLIANCE COMPANY
(Division Sunbeam Corporation)
2001 South York Road
Oak Brook, IL 60521
W. A. Crews

THE TAPPAN CO.
Tappan Park
Mansfield, OH 44901
D. C. Blasius

THERMADOR/WASTE KING
(Division of Norris Industries)
5119 District Boulevard
Los Angeles, CA 90040
Anthony A. Celio

HOUSEHOLD APPLIANCES

WARING PRODUCTS DIV. DYNAMICS CORP.
 OF AMERICA
Route 44
New Hartford, CT 06057
Robert C. Current, Jr.

WEST BEND CO.
(Affiliate of Dart Industries
 Inc.)
400 Washington
West Bend, WI 53095
E. M. Davis

WHIRLPOOL CORPORATION
Benton Harbor, MI 49022
Herb Anspach

TIRES, TUBES, RUBBER MOLDED PRODUCTS & PLASTICS

AMERACE CORPORATION
555 Fifth Avenue
New York, NY 10017
George S. Deutsch

AMERICAN BILTRITE INC.
575 Technology Square
Cambridge, MA 02139
George Safiol

THE ARMSTRONG RUBBER CO.
500 Sargent Drive
New Haven, CT 06507
James A. Walsh

BANDAG INC.
Bandag World Headquarters
Bandag Center, Muscatine, IA 52761
Harker Collins

CADILLAC PLASTIC & CHEMICAL CO.
(Division of Dayco Corp.)
P. O. Box 810
Detroit, MI 48232
W. D. Benkelman

CARLISLE CORPORATION
1700 DuBois Tower, 511 Walnut St.
Cincinnati, OH 45202
Malcolm C. Myers

TIRES, TUBES, RUBBER MOLDED PRODUCTS & PLASTICS

THE COOPER TIRE COMPANY
(Division of Cooper Tire & Rubber
 Co.)
Lima & Western Avenues
Findlay, OH 45840
W. T. Fitzgerald

DAYCO CORPORATION
333 West 1st Street
Dayton, OH 45402
Ernest F. Dourlet

THE DAYTON TIRE & RUBBER CO.
(Division of Firestone Tire &
 Rubber Co.)
2342 Riverview Avenue
Dayton, OH 45407
J. R. Thomas

DUNLOP TIRE & RUBBER CORP.
(Executive Offices & Tire Div.)
P. O. Box 1109
Buffalo, NY 14240
A. N. Procter

THE FIRESTONE TIRE & RUBBER CO.
1200 Firestone Parkway
Akron, OH 44317
Mario A. Di Federico

THE GATES RUBBER COMPANY
999 South Broadway
Denver, CO 80217
Charles C. Gates

THE GENERAL TIRE & RUBBER CO.
One General Street
Akron, OH 44329
M. G. O'Neil

THE B F GOODRICH COMPANY
500 South Main
Akron, OH 44318
J. D. Ong

THE GOODYEAR TIRE & RUBBER COMPANY
1144 East Market
Akron, OH 44316
J. H. Gerstenmaier

TIRES, TUBES, RUBBER MOLDED PRODUCTS & PLASTICS

MC CREARY TIRE & RUBBER CO.
Box 749
Indiana, PA 15701
H. C. McCreary

MOLDED FIBER GLASS COMPANIES
P.O. Box 675, 1315 W. 47th Street
Ashtabula, OH 44004
Richard S. Morrison

THE STANDARD PRODUCTS CO.
2130 West 110th
Cleveland, OH 44102
J. S. Reid, Jr.

TOILETRIES AND COSMETICS

ALBERTO-CULVER COMPANY
2525 Armitage Avenue
Melrose Park, IL 60160
Leonard H. Lavin

ALMAY, INC.
562 Fifth Avenue
New York, NY 10036
George Underwood

AMERICAN SAFETY RAZOR CO.
(Division of Philip Morris, Inc.)
Razor Blade Lane
Verona, VA 24482
John R. Baker

JOHN H. BRECK, INC.
(Subsidiary of American Cyanamid Co.)
859 Berdan Avenue
Wayne, NJ 07470
J. H. Dietze

BRISTOL-MYERS COMPANY
345 Park Avenue
New York, NY 10022
H. Sokol

CARTER-WALLACE, INC.
767 Fifth Avenue
New York, NY 10022
H. H. Hoyt, Jr.

TOILETRIES AND COSMETICS

CHANEL, INC.
9 West 57th Street
New York, NY 10019
Mark Baccash

CHARLES OF THE RITZ GROUP LTD.
(Subsidiary of Squibb Corp.)
40 West 57th Street
New York, NY 10019
Martin Schmidt

CHESEBROUGH-POND'S INC.
33 Benedict Place
Greenwich, CT 06830
R. E. Ward

CHRISTIAN DIOR PERFUMES CORPORATION
9 West 57th Street
New York, NY 10019
Pierre Rogers

COLGATE-PALMOLIVE COMPANY
300 Park Avenue
New York, NY 10022
Keith Crane

CONAIR CORPORATION
11 Executive Avenue
Edison, NJ 08817
L. P. Rizzuto

COSMAIR, INC.
530 Fifth Avenue
New York, NY 10036
Jean Caste

ESTEE LAUDER INC.
767 Fifth Avenue
New York, NY 10022
Leonard Lauder

EVYAN PERFUMES, INC.
350 East 35th
New York, NY 10016
Dr. W. Langer

FABERGE, INCORPORATED
1345 Avenue of the Americas
New York, NY 10019
Richard Barrie

TOILETRIES AND COSMETICS

THE GILLETTE COMPANY
Prudential Tower Building
Boston, MA 02199
Stephen J. Griffin

JOHNSON PRODUCTS CO. INC.
8522 South Lafayette Avenue
Chicago, IL 60620
George E. Johnson

MAX FACTOR & CO.
(Subsidiary of Norton Simon Inc.)
1655 North McCadden Place
Hollywood, CA 90028
Samuel Kalish

MAYBELLINE CO.
(Subsidiary of Plough, Inc.)
3030 Jackson Avenue
Memphis, TN 38151
David Brittain

THE MENNEN COMPANY
Hanover Avenue
Morristown, NJ 07960
L. Donald Horne

NOXELL CORPORATION
11050 York Road, P.O. Box 1799
Baltimore, MD 21203
George L. Bunting, Jr.

REVLON, INC.
767 Fifth Avenue
New York, NY 10022
Michel Bergerac

SCANNON LTD.
666 Fifth Avenue
New York, NY 10019
Bent Rasmussen

SEA & SKI CORPORATION
(Subsidiary of Smith Kline Corp.)
1500 Spring Garden Street
Philadelphia, PA 19101
Samuel Rulon-Miller

TOILETRIES AND COSMETICS

SHULTON, INC.
(Subsidiary of American Cyanamid Co.)
697 Route 46
Clifton, NJ 07015
A. Munsell

TAMPAX INCORPORATED
5 Dakota Drive
Lake Success, NY 11040
E. Russell Sprague

TELEDYNE WATER PIK
1730 East Prospect Street
Fort Collins, CO 80521
A. E. Rouse

THE WELLA CORPORATION
524 Grand Avenue
Englewood, NJ 07631
George Megerle

YARDLEY OF LONDON, INC.
(Subsidiary of Jovan, Inc.)
1555 Roadhaven Drive
Stone Mountain, GA 30083
William D. Hunt

TRAVEL & TRANSPORTATION

AIR CANADA
600 Madison Avenue
New York, NY 10022
J. P. Labrie

ALLEGHENY AIRLINES, INC.
Washington National Airport
Washington, D. C. 20001
Edwin I. Colodny

AMERICAN AIRLINES, INC.
633 Third Avenue
New York, NY 10017
Albert V. Casey

AMERICAN EXPRESS COMPANY
American Express Plaza
New York, NY 10004
R. H. Morley

TRAVEL & TRANSPORTATION

ASK MR. FOSTER TRAVEL SERVICE, INC.
7833 Haskell Avenue
Van Nuys, CA 91406
John A. Ueberroth

ATCHISON, TOPEKA & SANTA FE RAILWAY CO.
(Subsidiary of Santa Fe Industries, Inc.)
Railway Exchange, 80 E. Jackson
Chicago, IL 60604
L. Cena

ATLAS VAN LINES, INC.
1212 St. George Road
Evansville, IN 47711
Robert R. C. Miller

AVIS RENT A CAR SYSTEM, INC.
(Subsidiary of Norton Simon, Inc.)
1114 Avenue of the Americas
New York, NY 10036
C. M. Marshall

BRANIFF INTERNATIONAL
Braniff Tower, Exchange Park
Dallas, TX 75235
Russell Thayer

BUDGET RENT-A-CAR CORP.
(Subsidiary of Transamerica Corp.)
35 East Wacker Drive
Chicago, IL 60601
Morris Belzberg

CHICAGO, MILWAUKEE, ST. PAUL AND PACIFIC RAILROAD
516 West Jackson Boulevard
Chicago, IL 60606
Worthington L. Smith

CONTINENTAL AIR LINES, INC.
Los Angeles International Airport
Los Angeles, CA 90009
Alexander Damm

CUNARD LINE LTD.
555 Fifth Avenue
New York, NY 10017
George Law

TRAVEL & TRANSPORTATION

DELTA AIR LINES
Atlanta Airport
Atlanta, GA 30320
David C. Garrett, Jr.

EASTERN AIR LINES, INC.
Miami International Airport
Miami, FL 33148
Frank Borman

EMERY AIR FREIGHT CORP.
Wilton, CT 06897
J. C. Emery, Jr.

FLAGSHIP CRUISES
(Agents for Flagship Cruises Liberia Ltd.)
522 Fifth Avenue
New York, NY 10036
Oivind Lorentzen, Jr.

GRAY LINE SIGHTSEEING ASSOCIATION, INC.
7 West 51st Street
New York, NY 10019
Patrick Sheridan

GREYHOUND LINES, INC.
Greyhound Tower
Phoenix, AZ 85077
H. J. Lesko

HAWAIIAN AIRLINES, INC.
P. O. Box 30008
Honolulu International Airport
Honolulu, HI 96820
John H. Magoon, Jr.

THE HERTZ CORPORATION
(Subsidiary of RCA Corp.)
660 Madison Avenue
New York, NY 10021
Frank A. Olson

HOLLAND AMERICA CRUISES
Two Pennsylvania Plaza
New York, NY 10001
John R. Berry

TRAVEL & TRANSPORTATION

LAKER AIRWAYS
P. O. Box I, JKF Airport
Jamaica, NY 11430
Freddie Laker

MOORE-MC CORMACK LINES INCORPORATED
P. O. Box 2055, Airport Mail Facility
Miami, FL 33159
Lewis B. Maytag

NATIONAL CAR RENTAL SYSTEM, INC.
5501 Grand Valley Drive
Minneapolis, MN 55437
J. W. James

NORTH CENTRAL AIRLINES
7500 Northliner Drive
Minneapolis, MN 55450
Bernard Sweet

NORTHWEST ORIENT AIRLINES
(Division of Northwest Airlines, Inc., Minneapolis/St. Paul International Airport)
St. Paul, MN 55111
M. Joseph Lapensky

NORWEGIAN CARIBBEAN LINES
One Biscayne Tower
Miami, FL 33131
Thomas F. Simpson

OZARK AIR LINES, INC.
P.O. Box 10007, Lambert Field
St. Louis, MO 63145
Edward J. Crane

PACIFIC SOUTHWEST AIRLINES
3225 North Harbor Drive
San Diego, CA 92101
William R. Shimp

PAN AMERICAN WORLD AIRWAYS
Pan Am Building
New York, NY 10017
F. C. Wiser, Jr.

PIEDMONT AVIATION, INC.
Smith Reynolds Airport
Winston-Salem, NC 27102
William G. McGee

TRAVEL & TRANSPORTATION

PRINCESS CRUISES INC.
2020 Avenue of the Stars
Los Angeles, CA 90067
Stanley B. McDonald

ROYAL VIKING LINE
(Affiliate of Royal Viking Line A/S, Oslo, Norway)
One Embarcadero Center
San Francisco, CA 94116
Warren S. Titus

SITMAR CRUISES
10100 Santa Monica Boulevard
Los Angeles, CA 90067
John P. Bland

SOUTHERN AIRWAYS INC.
Atlanta Airport
Atlanta, GA 30320
T. A. Wiley, Jr.

TRAILWAYS, INC.
(Subsidiary of Holiday Inns, Inc.)
1512 Commerce Street
Dallas, TX 75201
J. Kevin Murphy

TRANS WORLD AIRLINES INC.
605 Third Avenue
New York, NY 10016
C. E. Meyer, Jr.

UNITED AIRLINES
(Executive Office-Mailing Address, P.O. Box 66100, Chicago, IL 60666)
1200 Algonquin Road
Elk Grove Village, IL 60007
R. J. Ferris

UNITED STATES LINES, INC.
1 Broadway
New York, NY 10004
E. J. Heine, Jr.

WESTERN AIR LINES, INC.
6060 Avion Drive
Los Angeles, CA 90045
Dominic P. Renda

Chapter 6: THE BETTER BUSINESS BUREAU

In this section we will look at what the Better Business Bureau (BBB) can and cannot do to help you with your consumer complaints. Although the BBB has no legal jurisdiction, it is often quite successful in dealing with consumer complaints, and it should be one of the first places to contact.

The BBB is also useful in helping you establish the reliability of local businesses or organizations. For instance, suppose your house needs a new roof and you are not sure which roofing firm to use. Call the BBB and request information on several local firms. The BBB can tell you how dependable the company is, whether they handle complaints in a reliable way, the length of time they have been in business, and the number of unsolved complaints against the company.

The BBB also keeps tabs on advertising to see that products or services are not advertised in a misleading way.

If you have a complaint about a local business or organization, the BBB will advise you on how to seek further action. If the BBB decides it can help with your complaint, they will ask that you send the complaint to them in writing. Then they will contact the party involved and act on your behalf.

The BBB can also provide arbitration to help settle a complaint. This program was recently introduced by the Council of Better Business Bureaus. It is available at many BBB's across the country, so when making a complaint with your local BBB, be sure to ask if they provide this service. Arbitration is used after all other ways have failed to settle a dispute. If you have a complaint and have not been able to get satisfaction from the firm on your own, you ask the local BBB to try on your behalf. If the BBB is also unsuccessful, they then offer to provide arbitration. If you and the businessman agree to accept the arbitration results, you would both sign an agreement stating this. This agreement is binding.

The BBB then helps to pick an arbitrator, or disinterested third party, who is acceptable to both you and the businessman. Both of you may use the services of a lawyer and provide witnesses to give evidence. The subject of the complaint, the product or repair job, will be inspected by the arbitrator. All these proceedings are held in an informal atmosphere. Finally the arbitrator will make a decision or give an award to settle the matter. The arbitration program provides the consumer with an inexpensive and less time-consuming method of getting satisfaction for his complaints.

Now we'll talk about those things that the BBB cannot do to help the consumer.

The BBB will not make judgments about specific brands of merchandise. It might give general information, for example, on the pros and cons of electric versus gas dryers, but it will not mention any brand names.

The BBB also will not become involved in disputes between a

seller and buyer concerning the cost of services or products. The exception is if there is evidence that the consumer is the victim of fraud or misleading advertising.

The arbitration program mentioned above is an informal method of settling disputes. The BBB does not give advice of a formal legal nature. It will only provide facts, and it is up to the consumer to make decisions and draw conclusions concerning local firms based on those facts.

There are over 140 BBB's in the U. S., and the following list, arranged by state, gives the address and phone number of the one nearest you. If you live in a state that does not have a local BBB, go to your local Chamber of Commerce with your complaint. If you have a complaint against a local BBB, you may make that complaint to:

>   The Council of Better Business Bureaus, Inc.
>   1150 17th Street, N.W.
>   Washington, D.C. 20036
>   (202) 467-5200

> or

>   The Council of Better Business Bureaus, Inc.
>   845 Third Avenue
>   New York, NY 10022
>   (212) 754-3200

STATE OFFICES

ALABAMA

Birmingham

The BBB, Inc.
2026 Second Avenue, North
Suite 2303
Birmingham, Alabama 35203
(205) 323-6127

Huntsville

BBB of North Alabama, Inc.
102 Clinton Avenue, West
Terry Hutchins Building
Suite 512
Huntsville, Alabama 35801
(205) 533-1640

Mobile

BBB of South Alabama-NW Florida, Inc.
307 Van Antwerp Building
Mobile, Alabama 36602
(205) 433-5494

ARIZONA

Phoenix

BBB of Maricopa County, Inc.
718 West Glenrosa
Phoenix, Arizona 85013
(602) 264-1721

Tucson

BBB of Tucson, Inc.
100 East Alameda Street
Suite 407
Tucson, Arizona 85701
(602) 624-2356

ARKANSAS

Little Rock

BBB of Arkansas, Inc.
1216 South University
Little Rock, Arkansas 72204
(501) 664-7274

CALIFORNIA

Bakersfield

BBB of South Central California, Inc.
705 Eighteenth Street
Bakersfield, California 93301
(805) 322-2074

Colton (formerly San Bernardino)

BBB of Inland Cities
1265 North La Cadena
Colton, California 92324
(714) 825-7280
(Branch Office: Palm Desert)

Fresno

BBB of Central California, Inc.
413 T W Patterson Building
Fresno, California 93721
(209) 268-6424

Long Beach

BBB of Long Beach
130 Pine Avenue
Long Beach, California 90802
(213) 437-0618
(Branch of BBB Los Angeles)

Los Angeles

BBB of Los Angeles/Orange County
417 South Hill Street-Suite 575
Los Angeles, California 90013
(213) 627-6305
(Branch Offices: Long Beach and
Orange)

Oakland

BBB of Metropolitan Oakland, Inc.
360 22nd Street
El Dorado Building
Oakland, California 94612
(415) 839-5900

Orange

BBB of Orange County
1818 West Chapman Avenue
Orange, California 92668
(714) 633-9662
(Branch Office of BBB Los Angeles)

Palm Desert

BBB of Palm Desert
74-273½ Highway 111
Palm Desert, California 92260
(714) 346-2014
(Branch Office of BBB Colton)

Sacramento

BBB of Sacramento, Inc.
1401 21st Street-Suite 305
Sacramento, California 95814
(916) 443-6843

Salinas

BBB of Santa Clara Valley, Ltd.
423 Pajaro Street
Salinas, California 93901
(408) 757-2022
(Branch Office of San Jose)

San Bernardino (see Colton)

San Diego

BBB of San Diego, Ltd.
4310 Orange Avenue
San Diego, California 92105
(714) 283-3927

San Francisco

BBB of San Francisco, Ltd.
414 Mason Street-Suite 500
San Francisco, California 94102
(415) 398-4300
(Branch Office: San Rafael)

San Jose

BBB of Santa Clara Valley, Ltd.
P. O. Box 8110
San Jose, California 95155
(408) 298-5880
(Branch Office: Santa Cruz)

San Luis Obispo

BBB of the Tri-Counties
P. O. Box 1146
San Luis Obispo, California 93406
(805) 541-1325
(Branch Office of BBB Santa Barbara.
 All mail to Santa Barbara.)

San Mateo

BBB of San Mateo County, Inc.
P.O. Box 294, 20 North San Mateo Drive
San Mateo, California 94401
(415) 347-1251

San Rafael

BBB of San Francisco, Ltd.
1010 B Street-Room 310
San Rafael, California 94901
(415) 453-9442
(Branch Office of BBB San Francisco)

Santa Barbara

BBB of the Tri-Counties
P. O. Box 746
Santa Barbara, California 93102
(805) 963-8657
(Branch Office: San Luis Obispo)

Santa Cruz

BBB of Santa Clara Valley, Inc.
5730 Soquel Drive
Soquel, California 95073
(408) 476-6144

Stockton

BBB of San Joaquin County, Inc.
Bank of America Bldg.-Room 420
343 East Main Street
Stockton, California 95202
(209) 948-4880

Vallejo

North Bay BBB, Inc.
1523 Tennessee Street
Vallejo, California 94590
(707) 643-5087

COLORADO

Denver

Rocky Mountain BBB, Inc.
841 Delaware Street
Denver, Colorado 80204
(303) 629-1036

CONNECTICUT

Bridgeport

BBB of Southwestern Connecticut, Inc.
144 Golden Hill Street-Suite 603
Bridgeport, Connecticut 06604
(203) 368-6538

Hartford

BBB of Greater Hartford, Inc.
250 Constitution Plaza
Hartford, Connecticut 06103
(203) 249-5884

New Haven

BBB of Greater New Haven, Inc.
152 Temple Street-P.O.Box 1445
New Haven, Connecticut 06506
(203) 787-5788

DELAWARE

Milford

Kent-Sussex Better Business Bureau
20 South Walnut Street
Milford, Delaware 19963
(302) 422-6300 & 856-6969

Wilmington

BBB of Delaware, Inc.
1901-B West Eleventh Street
P. O. Box 4085
Wilmington, Delaware 19807
(302) 652-3833

DISTRICT OF COLUMBIA

Washington

BBB of Metropolitan Washington, D.C.
507 Perpetual Building
1111 "E" Street, N.W.
Washington, D. C. 20004
(202) 393-8000
(Branch Office: Bethesda, Maryland)

FLORIDA

Miami

BBB of South Florida, Inc.
8600 N.E. Second Avenue
Miami, Florida 33138
(305) 757-1568

West Palm Beach

BBB of Palm Beach County, Inc.
Pan American Building-Suite 321
West Palm Beach, Florida 33401
(305) 832-6418

GEORGIA

Atlanta

BBB of Metropolitan Atlanta, Inc.
212 Healey Building
57 Forsyth Street, N.W.
Atlanta, Georgia 30303
(404) 688-4910

Augusta

BBB of Augusta, Inc.
P. O. Box 2085
360 Bay Street, Room 100
Augusta, Georgia 30903
(404) 722-1574

Columbus

BBB of West Georgia-East Alabama, Inc.
P. O. Box 1218
Columbus, Georgia 31902
(404) 327-2671

Savannah

BBB of Coastal Empire, Inc.
1310 Abercorn Street-P.O.Box 10006
Savannah, Georgia 31402
(912) 234-5336

HAWAII

Honolulu

BBB of Hawaii, Inc.
677 Ala Moana Boulevard-Suite 602
Honolulu, Hawaii 96813
(808) 531-8131

Maui

BBB of Hawaii, Inc.
P. O. Box 311
Kahului, Hawaii 96732
(808) 877-4000
(Branch Office: BBB Honolulu)

IDAHO

Boise

BBB of Treasure Valley, Inc.
709½ Idaho Street
Boise, Idaho 83702
(208) 342-4649

ILLINOIS

Chicago

BBB of Metropolitan Chicago, Inc.
430 North Michigan Avenue
Chicago, Illinois 60611
(312) 467-4400

Peoria

BBB of Central Illinois, Inc.
109 S.W. Jefferson St.-Suite 305
Peoria, Illinois 61602
(309) 673-5194

INDIANA

Elkhart

Better Business Bureau
118 South Second St., P.O. Box 405
Elkhart, Indiana 46514
(219) 523-4545

Fort Wayne

BBB of Northeastern Indiana, Inc.
716 South Barr Street
Fort Wayne, Indiana 46802
(219) 423-4433

Gary

BBB of Northwest Indiana, Inc.
2500 West Ridge Road
Calumet Turnpike
Gary, Indiana 46408
(219) 980-1511

Indianapolis

Central Indiana BBB, Inc.
30 East Georgia Street
Indianapolis, Indiana 46204
(317) 637-3371

South Bend

BBB of South Bend-Mishawaka
 Area, Inc.
320 West Jefferson Blvd., St. 303
South Bend, Indiana 46601
(219) 234-0183

IOWA

Des Moines

BBB of Des Moines, Inc.
234 Insurance Exchange Building
Des Moines, Iowa 50309
(515) 243-8137

Sioux City

Siouxland BBB, Inc.
731 Badgerow Building
622 Fourth Street
Sioux City, Iowa 51101
(712) 252-4501

KANSAS

Topeka

BBB of Northeast Kansas, Inc.
Suite 24, Ramada Inn
501 Jefferson
Topeka, Kansas 66607
(913) 232-0454

Wichita

BBB, Inc.
306 Insurance Building
Wichita, Kansas 67202
(316) 263-3146

KENTUCKY

Lexington

BBB of Central Kentucky, Inc.
117 West Second Street
Lexington, Kentucky 40507
(606) 252-4492

Louisville

BBB of Greater Louisville, Inc.
312 West Chestnut Street
Louisville, Kentucky 40202
(502) 583-6546

LOUISIANA

Baton Rouge

BBB of Baton Rouge Area, Inc.
200 Laurel Street
Baton Rouge, Louisiana 70801
(504) 344-8551

Lafayette

BBB of Arcadiana, Inc.
431 South Buchanan Street
Lafayette, Louisiana 70501
(318) 234-8341

Lake Charles

BBB of Southwest Louisiana, Inc.
114 Ryan Street
Lake Charles, Louisiana 70601
(318) 433-6133

Monroe

BBB of Northeast Louisiana, Inc.
102 South Grand Street
Monroe, Louisiana 71201
(318) 387-4600

New Orleans

BBB of Greater New Orleans Area, Inc.
301 Camp Street, Suite 403
New Orleans, Louisiana 70130
(504) 581-6222

Shreveport

BBB of Shreveport & Bossier, Inc.
306 LBT Milam Building
Shreveport, Louisiana 71101
(318) 221-8352

MARYLAND

Baltimore

BBB of Baltimore, Inc.
401 North Howard Street
Baltimore, Maryland 21201
(301) 685-6986

Bethesda

BBB of Montgomery County
316 Perpetual Building
7401 Wisconsin Avenue
Bethesda, Maryland 20014
(301) 656-7000
(Branch Office of BBB Washington, D.C.)

MASSACHUSETTS

Boston

BBB of Eastern Massachusetts, Inc.
150 Tremont Street
Boston, Massachusetts 02111
(617) 482-9151
(Branch Office: Cape Cod)

Cape Cod

Cape Cod BBB
233 Barnstable Road
Hyannis, Massachusetts 02601
(617) 771-3022
(Branch Office of BBB Boston)

Springfield

BBB of Western Massachusetts
145 State Street
Springfield, Massachusetts 01103
(413) 734-3114

Worcester

BBB of Central New England, Inc.
50 Franklin Street
Worcester, Massachusetts 01608
(617) 755-2548

MICHIGAN

Detroit

BBB of Metropolitan Detroit, Inc.
150 Michigan Avenue
Detroit, Michigan 48226
(313) 962-0550

Grand Rapids

BBB of Greater Grand Rapids, Inc.
1 Peoples Building
Grand Rapids, Michigan 49502
(616) 774-8236

MINNESOTA

St. Paul

BBB of Minnesota
1745 University Avenue
St. Paul, Minnesota 55104
(612) 646-4631
(Merger of St. Paul and Minneapolis)

MISSISSIPPI

Jackson

BBB of Mississippi, Inc.
621 Barnett Bldg., P.O.Box 2090
Jackson, Mississippi 39205
(601) 948-4732

MISSOURI

Kansas City

BBB of Greater Kansas City, Inc.
906 Grand Avenue
Kansas City, Missouri 64106
(816) 421-7800

St. Louis

BBB of Greater St. Louis, Inc.
915 Olive Street
St. Louis, Missouri 63101
(314) 241-3100

Springfield

BBB of Southwest Missouri, Inc.
P.O.Box 4331, Glenstone Station
Springfield, Missouri 65804
(417) 862-9231

NEBRASKA

Lincoln

Cornhusker BBB, Inc.
411 South 13th Street, Suite 320
Lincoln, Nebraska 68508
(402) 467-5261

Omaha

BBB of Omaha, Inc.
Redick Tower Building
15th & Harney Street
Omaha, Nebraska 68102
(402) 346-3033

NEVADA

Las Vegas

BBB of Southern Nevada, Inc.
538 East Sahara Avenue
Las Vegas, Nevada 89105
(702) 732-2002

Reno

BBB of Northern Nevada, Inc.
1890 Locust St., P.O. Box 2932
Reno, Nevada 89505
(702) 322-0657

NEW HAMPSHIRE

Concord

BBB of the Granite State
72 North Main Street
Concord, New Hampshire 03301
(603) 224-1991

NEW JERSEY

Collingswood

BBB of South Jersey, Inc.
P. O. Box 303
Collingswood, New Jersey 08108
(609) 854-8467
(Branch Office: Ocean County)

Newark

BBB of Greater Newark, Inc.
15 Washington Street
Newark, New Jersey 07102
(201) 828-5500
(Branch Office of BBB Metro NY)

New Brunswick

BBB of New Brunswick
390 George Street
New Brunswick, New Jersey 08901
(201) 643-3025
(Branch Office of BBB Trenton)

Ocean City

Ocean County BBB
1721 Route 37 East
Toms River, New Jersey 08753
(201) 341-8202
(Branch Office of BBB Collingswood)

Paramus

BBB of Bergen, Passaic & Rockland
 Counties
2 Forest Avenue
Paramus, New Jersey 07652
(201) 845-4044
(Branch Office of BBB Metro NY)

Trenton

BBB of Central New Jersey, Inc.
25 Texas Avenue
Trenton, New Jersey 08638
(609) 883-6966
(Branch Office: New Brunswick)

NEW MEXICO

Albuquerque

BBB of New Mexico, Inc.
154-156 Washington Street
Albuquerque, New Mexico 87108
(505) 266-5611

NEW YORK

Buffalo

BBB of Western New York, Inc.
238 Main Street
Buffalo, New York 14202
(716) 856-7180
(Branch Office: Buffalo)

BBB of Western New York, Inc.
1490 Jefferson Avenue
Buffalo, New York 14208
(716) 856-7180
(Branch Office of BBB Buffalo)

Long Island

Long Island BBB
435 Old County Road
Westbury, New York 11590
(516) 334-7662
(Branch Office of BBB Metro NY)

New York

BBB of Metro N. Y., Inc.
110 Fifth Avenue
New York, New York 10011
(212) 989-6160
(Branch Offices: New York City, Long Island, White Plains, Newark, New Jersey, and Paramus, New Jersey)

New York (Harlem)

BBB of Harlem
2090 Seventh Avenue
New York, New York 10027
(212) 749-7106
(Branch Office of BBB Metro NY)

Rochester

BBB of Rochester, Inc.
731 Sibley Tower Building
Rochester, New York 14604
(716) 546-6776

Syracuse

BBB of Syracuse & Central N. Y.
120 East Washington Street
Syracuse, New York 13202
(315) 479-6635

Utica

BBB of the Mohawk Valley, Inc.
209 Elizabeth Street
Utica, New York 13501
(315) 724-3129

White Plains

BBB of Westchester, Putnam & Duchess Counties
158 Westchester Avenue
White Plains, New York 10601
(914) 428-1230
(Branch Office of BBB Metro NY)

NORTH CAROLINA

Asheville

The BBB of the Asheville-Western North Carolina, Inc.
29½ Page Avenue
Asheville, North Carolina 28801
(704) 253-2892

Charlotte

Piedmont BBB, Inc.
312 City National Bank Building
Charlotte, North Carolina 28202
(704) 332-5106

Greensboro

BBB of Central North Carolina, Inc.
225 North Greene St., P.O. Box 2400
Greensboro, North Carolina 27402
(919) 273-2531

Research Triangle Park

Triangle Cities BBB
P. O. Box 12033
Research Triangle Park, North Carolina 27709
(919) 549-8221

Winston-Salem

The BBB, Inc.
914 First Union National Bank Bldg.
Winston-Salem, North Carolina 27101
(919) 725-8348

OHIO

Akron

BBB of Akron, Inc.
P.O. Box 1884, 84 West Bowery Street
Akron, Ohio 44309
(216) 525-4590

Canton

BBB of Stark County, Inc.
203 Market Avenue, South
Harvard Building
Canton, Ohio 44702
(216) 454-9401

Cincinnati

Cincinnati BBB, Inc.
26 East Sixth Street
Cincinnati, Ohio 45202
(513) 421-3015

Cleveland

The Cleveland BBB
1720 Keith Building
Cleveland, Ohio 44115
(216) 241-7678

Columbus

BBB of Central Ohio, Inc.
71 East State Street
Columbus, Ohio 43215
(614) 221-6336

Dayton

BBB of Dayton/Miami Valley, Inc.
7 East Fourth Street-Suite 2000
Dayton, Ohio 45402
(513) 222-5825

Toledo

BBB of Toledo, Inc.
214 Board of Trade Building
Toledo, Ohio 43604
(419) 241-6276

Youngstown

BBB of Mahoning Valley, Inc.
903 Mahoning Bank Building
23 Central Square
Youngstown, Ohio 44503
(216) 744-8938

OKLAHOMA

Oklahoma City

BBB of Central Oklahoma, Inc.
208 Leonhardt Building
Oklahoma City, Oklahoma 73102
(405) 239-6081

Tulsa

BBB of Tulsa, Inc.
4867 South Sheridan-Suite 714
Tulsa, Oklahoma 74145
(918) 664-1266

OREGON

Portland

Portland BBB, Inc.
623 Corbett Building
Portland, Oregon 97204
(503) 226-3981

PENNSYLVANIA

Philadelphia

BBB of Eastern Pennsylvania
P. O. Box 1466
Philadelphia, Pennsylvania 19105
(215) 923-7636

Pittsburgh

BBB of Western Pennsylvania, Inc.
Grant Building
Pittsburgh, Pennsylvania 15219
(412) 281-2260

Scranton

BBB of Northeastern Pennsylvania,
 Inc.
210 Mears Building
146 North Washington Avenue
Scranton, Pennsylvania 18503
(717) 342-9129

RHODE ISLAND

Providence

BBB of Rhode Island, Inc.
248 Weybosset Street
Providence, Rhode Island 02903
(401) 272-9800

TENNESSEE

Chattanooga

BBB of Greater Chattanooga, Inc.
11 West Eighth Street
Chattanooga Bank Building
Chattanooga, Tennessee 37402
(615) 266-6144

Knoxville

BBB of Greater Knoxville/East
 Tennessee, Inc.
P. O. Box 3608
Knoxville, Tennessee 37917
(615) 522-2139

Memphis

Memphis Area BBB, Inc.
100 North Main Building-Suite 1210
Memphis, Tennessee 38103
(901) 525-8501

Nashville

BBB of Nashville/Middle Tennessee,
 Inc.
506 Nashville City Bank Building
Nashville, Tennessee 37201
(615) 254-5872

TEXAS

Abilene

BBB of Abilene, Inc.
P.O. Box 3275, 325 Hickory Street
Abilene, Texas 79604
(915) 677-8071

Amarillo

BBB of the Golden Spread
518 Amarillo Building
Amarillo, Texas 79101
(806) 374-3735

Austin

BBB of Austin, Inc.
American Bank Tower-Suite 720
Austin, Texas 78701
(512) 476-6943

Beaumont

BBB of Southeast Texas, Inc.
Goodhue Building-Suite 405
Beaumont, Texas 77701
(713) 835-5348

Bryan

BBB of Brazos Valley, Inc.
307 Varisco Building
Bryan, Texas 77801
(713) 823-8148

Corpus Christi

BBB of Corpus Christi, Inc.
403 N. Shoreline Dr.-Suite 100
Corpus Christi, Texas 78401
(512) 888-5555

Dallas

BBB of Metropolitan Dallas, Inc.
1511 Bryan Street
Dallas, Texas 75201
(214) 747-8891

El Paso

BBB of El Paso, Inc.
2501 North Mesa Street-Suite 301
El Paso, Texas 79902
(915) 544-2420

Fort Worth

BBB of Fort Worth & Tarrant County
709 Sinclair Building
106 West Fifth Street
Fort Worth, Texas 76102
(817) 332-7585

Houston

BBB of Metropolitan Houston, Inc.
1212 Main Street-Suite 533
Houston, Texas 77002
(713) 224-6111

Lubbock

BBB of the South Plains, Inc.
P. O. Box 1178
Lubbock, Texas 79408
(806) 763-0459

Midland

BBB of the Permian Basin, Inc.
Air Terminal Bldg., P.O.Box 6006
Midland, Texas 79701
(915) 563-1880

San Antonio

BBB of San Antonio, Inc.
406 West Market Street-Suite 301
San Antonio, Texas 78205
(512) 225-5833

Waco

BBB of Waco, Inc.
608 New Road, P.O.Box 7203
Waco, Texas 76710
(817) 772-7530

UTAH

Salt Lake City

BBB of Greater Salt Lake, Inc.
1388 South Main
Salt Lake City, Utah 84115
(801) 487-4656

VIRGINIA

Norfolk

Tidewater BBB, Inc.
First & Merchants Bank Building
300 Main Street, East
Norfolk, Virginia 23510
(804) 627-5651

Richmond

BBB of Richmond, Inc.
4020 West Broad Street
Richmond, Virginia 23230
(804) 355-7902

Roanoke

BBB of Roanoke Valley, Inc.
646 A Crystal Tower
145 West Campbell Avenue, S.W.
Roanoke, Virginia 24011
(703) 342-3455

WASHINGTON

Seattle

BBB of Greater Seattle, Inc.
538 Denny Bldg., 2200 Sixth Ave.
Seattle, Washington 98121
(206) 622-8066

Spokane

BBB of Spokane, Inc.
514 Columbia Building
Spokane, Washington 99204
(509) 747-1155

Tacoma

Tacoma BBB, Inc.
824 Rust Building
Tacoma, Washington 98402
(206) 383-5561

Yakima

BBB of Central Washington, Inc.
P. O. Box 1584
Yakima, Washington 98907
(509) 248-1326

WISCONSIN

Milwaukee

BBB of Greater Milwaukee
174 West Wisconsin Ave.-Suite 300
Milwaukee, Wisconsin 53203
(414) 273-1600

Chapter 7: FEDERAL AGENCIES

The federal government, ever a complex beast, hasn't gotten any simpler in the past few years. During those same years, however, consumer activism has been on the rise, and the sounds of outrage have reached even into the winding halls of bureaucratic power in Washington, D. C. Better consumer laws are being enacted all the time, and old ones updated to ensure the plugging of loopholes. Most congressmen and senators are sensitive to constituent complaints about consumer issues, and even more sensitive to a complaint that tells of bad results or no results when complaining to a federal agency. The result of all this pressure has been to make the bureaucracy more responsive, too.

Sometimes, a consumer with an intransigent problem just gives up when he or she thinks about tackling the feds. But we're here to tell you that you shouldn't give up. Yes, there have been cases of unanswered complaints, and certainly cases in which a federal agency couldn't help. But there have also been times -- lots more than you might think -- when an agency of the federal government has swung into action on behalf of a citizen with a problem and cleared the way as only the federal government can, when it wants to.

First of all, it helps to know which agency is the right one to approach. This directory aims to provide you not just with the names and addresses of the big federal agencies that deal with consumer questions, but also an explanation of just when this particular agency can and can't do you some good. If you're still puzzled, you might consult the little-known but very helpful agency that's first on our list:

Federal Information Centers: These centers, located all around the country, are in business to provide you with information about the government, and to put you in touch with the particular part of our lumbering but well-intentioned ship of state that can help you out. Your question doesn't have to be about consumerism, or about the government; it can be about anything. Whether you're looking for a pamphlet on post-holes or an update on Uruguay, the information centers can tell you where to look. Not that each federal information center has all those facts at its collective fingertips, but it's their job to know who in the government does. If you want to know which federal agency can look into your consumer question, the information center is a good place to start looking. Not every city has a center, but some that don't have telephone tie-lines that you can use to call the nearest one.

ARIZONA

Federal Building
230 North First Avenue
Phoenix, Arizona 85025
(602) 261-3313

CALIFORNIA

Federal Building
300 North Los Angeles Street
Los Angeles, California 90012
(213) 688-3800

Federal Building
U. S. Courthouse
650 Capitol Mall
Sacramento, California 95814
(916) 449-3344

202 C Street
San Diego, California 92101
(714) 293-6030

Federal Building
U. S. Courthouse
450 Golden Gate Avenue
San Francisco, California 94101
(415) 566-6600

COLORADO

Federal Building
1961 Stout Street
Denver, Colorado 80202
(303) 837-3602

DISTRICT OF COLUMBIA

Seventh and D Streets, S.W.
Room 5716
Washington, D. C. 20407
(202) 755-8660

FLORIDA

Federal Building
51 Southwest First Avenue
Miami, Florida 33130
(305) 350-4155

GEORGIA

Federal Building
275 Peachtree Street, N.E.
Atlanta, Georgia 30303
(404) 526-6891

HAWAII

U. S. Post Office
Courthouse and Customhouse
335 Merchant Street
Honolulu, Hawaii 96813
(808) 546-8620

ILLINOIS

Everett McKinley Dirksen Building
219 South Dearborn Street
Chicago, Illinois 60604
(312) 353-4242

INDIANA

Federal Building
575 North Pennsylvania
Indianapolis, Indiana 46204
(317) 269-7373

KENTUCKY

Federal Building
600 Federal Place
Louisville, Kentucky 40202
(502) 582-6261

LOUISIANA

Federal Building
Room 1210
701 Loyola Avenue
New Orleans, Louisiana 70113
(504) 589-6696

MARYLAND

Federal Building
31 Hopkins Plaza
Baltimore, Maryland 21201
(301) 962-4980

MASSACHUSETTS

J.F.K. Federal Building
Cambridge Street
Lobby, First Floor
Boston, Massachusetts 02203
(617) 223-7121

MICHIGAN

Federal Building
U. S. Courthouse
231 West Lafayette Street
Detroit, Michigan 48226
(313) 226-7016

MINNESOTA

Federal Building
U. S. Courthouse
110 South Fourth Street
Minneapolis, Minnesota 55401
(612) 725-2073

MISSOURI

Federal Building
601 East Twelfth Street
Kansas City, Missouri 64106
(816) 374-2466

Federal Building
1520 Market Street
St. Louis, Missouri 63103
(314) 425-4106

NEBRASKA

Federal Building
U. S. Post Office and Courthouse
215 North 17th Street
Omaha, Nebraska 68102
(402) 221-3353

NEW JERSEY

Federal Building
970 Broad Street
Newark, New Jersey 17102
(201) 645-3600

NEW MEXICO

Federal Building
U. S. Courthouse
500 Gold Avenue, S.W.
Albuquerque, New Mexico 87101
(505) 766-3091

NEW YORK

Federal Building
111 West Huron Street
Buffalo, New York 14202
(716) 842-5770

Lobby, Federal Building
26 Federal Plaza
New York, New York 10007
(212) 264-4464

OHIO

Federal Building
550 Main Street
Cincinnati, Ohio 45202
(513) 684-2801

Federal Building
1240 East Ninth Street
Cleveland, Ohio 44199
(216) 522-4040

OKLAHOMA

U. S. Post Office and Courthouse
201 N. W. 3rd Street
Oklahoma City, Oklahoma 73102
(405) 231-4868

OREGON

Federal Building
1220 S. W. Third Avenue
Portland, Oregon 97204
(503) 221-2222

PENNSYLVANIA

Federal Building
600 Arch Street
Philadelphia, Pennsylvania 19106
(215) 597-7042

Federal Building
1000 Liberty Avenue
Pittsburgh, Pennsylvania 15222
(412) 644-3456

TENNESSEE

Clifford Davis Federal Building
167 Main Street North
Memphis, Tennessee 38103
(901) 534-3285

TEXAS

Fritz Garland Lanham Federal Building
819 Taylor Street
Fort Worth, Texas 76102
(817) 334-3624

Federal Building
U. S. Courthouse
515 Rusk Avenue
Houston, Texas 77002
(713) 226-5711

UTAH

Federal Building
U. S. Post Office, Courthouse
125 South State Street
Salt Lake City, Utah 84138
(801) 524-5353

WASHINGTON

Federal Building
915 Second Avenue
Seattle, Washington 98174
(206) 442-0570

TIE-LINES FROM OTHER CITIES TO FEDERAL INFORMATION CENTERS

Akron, Ohio: 375-5475

Albany, New York: 463-4421

Austin, Texas: 472-5494

Birmingham, Alabama: 322-8591

Charlotte, North Carolina: 376-3600

Chattanooga, Tennessee: 265-8231

Colorado Springs, Colorado: 471-9491

Columbus, Ohio: 221-1014

Dallas, Texas: 749-2131

Dayton, Ohio: 223-7377

Des Moines, Iowa: 282-9091

Fort Lauderdale, Florida: 522-8531

Hartford, Connecticut: 527-2617

Jacksonville, Florida: 354-4756

Little Rock, Arkansas: 378-6177

Milwaukee, Wisconsin: 271-2273

Mobile, Alabama: 438-1421

New Haven, Connecticut: 624-4720

Ogden, Utah: 399-1347

Providence, Rhode Island: 331-5565

Pueblo, Colorado: 544-9523

Rochester, New York: 546-5075

San Antonio, Texas: 224-4471

San Jose, California: 375-7422

Santa Fe, New Mexico: 983-7743

Scranton, Pennsylvania: 346-7081

St. Joseph, Missouri: 233-8206

Syracuse, New York: 476-8545

Tacoma, Washington: 383-5230

Tampa, Florida: 229-7911

Toledo, Ohio: 244-8625

Topeka, Kansas: 232-7229   Tulsa, Oklahoma: 584-4193
Trenton, New Jersey: 396-4400   West Palm Beach, Florida: 833-7566
Tucson, Arizona: 622-1511   Wichita, Kansas: 263-6931

DEPARTMENT OF AGRICULTURE

There are two agencies of the USDA that are directly concerned with consumer problems. One is the Agricultural Marketing Service (AMS), which is the division responsible for the voluntary grading program. It's the AMS that determines if your eggs are Grade A or AA, and what categories many other products fit into. An agricultural product may have been graded by the AMS whether or not a grade denotation appears on the label. The AMS also circulates a monthly "Food Marketing Alert," which lists which foods will be in plentiful or short supply that month, as well as other market predictions and recipes to help consumers use the plentiful foods.

The Animal and Plant Health Inspection Service runs an inspection program to ensure the wholesomeness of meat and poultry, as well as plant products. The APHIS shares regional offices with the Agricultural Marketing Service as follows:

Northeast: Serves Connecticut, Delaware, Massachusetts, Maryland, Maine, New Hampshire, New Jersey, New York, Pennsylvania, Rhode Island, Washington, D. C. and West Virginia

Information Division, AMS
USDA
26 Federal Plaza
Room 1653
New York, New York 10007

Southeast: Serves Alabama, Florida, Georgia, Kentucky, Mississippi, North Carolina, South Carolina, Tennessee and Virginia

Information Division, AMS
USDA
1718 Peachtree Street, N.W.
Room 220
Atlanta, Georgia 30309

Midwest: Serves Iowa, Illinois, Indiana, Michigan, Minnesota, Missouri, Nebraska, North Dakota, Ohio, South Dakota and Wisconsin

Information Division, AMS
USDA
536 South Clark Street
Room 936
Chicago, Illinois 60605

Southwest: Serves Arkansas, Colorado, Kansas, Louisiana, New Mexico, Oklahoma and Texas

Information Division, AMS
USDA
1100 Commerce Street
Room 6040
Dallas, Texas 75202

Western: Serves Alaska, Arizona, California, Hawaii, Idaho, Montana, Nevada, Oregon, Utah, Washington and Wyoming

Information Division, AMS
USDA
630 Sansome Street
Room 702
San Francisco, California 94111

BUREAU OF ALCOHOL, TOBACCO AND FIREARMS

This agency has control over the ingredient labeling for alcohol, legal trade in firearms and criminal violations of firearms laws. If you have problems or questions about any of these things, address your letter or call to:

Bureau of Alcohol, Tobacco and Firearms
U. S. Treasury Department
Washington, D. C. 20226
(202) 961-7135

CIVIL AERONAUTICS BOARD

The CAB has jurisdiction over such problems as deceptive scheduling, rates, advertising, overbooking and handling of customer complaints by airlines. If you have tried and failed to get satisfaction from any CAB-regulated air carrier, address letters to the:

Office of the Consumer Advocate
Civil Aeronautics Board

1825 Connecticut Avenue, N.W.
Washington, D. C. 20428
(202) 382-7735

If you aren't sure whether your complaint can be brought before the board, address inquiries to:

Office of Public Affairs
Civil Aeronautics Board
1825 Connecticut Avenue, N.W.
Washington, D. C. 20428
(202) 382-6031

CONSUMER PRODUCT SAFETY COMMISSION

The CPSC has the authority to ban hazardous consumer products or to otherwise regulate so as to reduce the unreasonable risk of injury associated with these products. The CPSC sets safety standards, such as the standards for fire-preventive treatment of children's sleepwear, and may ban a product outright if it proves too dangerous. If you think you know of a product -- other than those under separate legislation, such as cars, drugs, firearms, and foods -- contact the nearest regional office of the CPSC. There are also two toll-free lines: In Maryland, call (800) 492-2937. Elsewhere, dial (800) 638-2666.

Regional offices of the CPSC:

Atlanta Area Office:
Consumer Product Safety Commission
1330 West Peachtree Street, N.W.
Atlanta, Georgia 30309
(404) 526-2231

Boston Area Office:
Consumer Product Safety Commission
100 Summer Street, 16th Floor
Boston, Massachusetts 02110
(617) 223-5576

Chicago Area Office:

Consumer Product Safety Commission
230 South Dearborn Street, Rm. 2945
Chicago, Illinois 60604
(312) 353-8260

Dallas Area Office:

Consumer Product Safety Commission
Room 410 C, 500 South Ervay
Dallas, Texas 75201
(214) 749-3871

Denver Area Office:

Consumer Product Safety Commission
Suite 938, Guaranty Bank Building
817 17th Street
Denver, Colorado 80202
(303) 837-2904

Kansas City Area Office:

Consumer Product Safety Commission
Suite 1500, Traders National Bank
 Building
1125 Grand Avenue
Kansas City, Missouri 64106
(816) 374-2034

Los Angeles Area Office:

Consumer Product Safety Commission
3660 Wilshire Boulevard, Suite 1100
Los Angeles, California 90010
(213) 688-7272

Minneapolis Area Office:

Consumer Product Safety Commission
Room 650, Federal Building
Fort Snelling
Twin Cities, Minnesota 55111
(612) 725-3424

New York Area Office:

Consumer Product Safety Commission
6 World Trade Center
Vesey Street, 6th Floor
New York, New York 10048
(212) 264-1134

Philadelphia Area Office:

Consumer Product Safety Commission
10th Floor, 400 Market Street
Philadelphia, Pennsylvania 19106
(215) 597-9105

San Francisco Area Office:

Consumer Product Safety Commission
Suite 500, 100 Pine Street
San Francisco, California 94111
(415) 556-1819

Seattle Area Office:

Consumer Product Safety Commission
Federal Building, Room 3240
915 Second Avenue
Seattle, Washington 98174
(206) 442-5276

DEPARTMENT OF TRANSPORTATION

The DOT is the overseer of all national transportation policies. If you have any transportation-related difficulty, from an unresolved complaint about a bus company to one about the condition of highways or railroad tracks, the DOT may be able to help you, or at least to tell you who can. If you have doubts or questions, write the:

Office of Consumer Affairs
U. S. Department of Transportation
Washington, D. C. 20590

You may be directed to one of the DOT's regional offices, or to some other agency, such as the CAB, more appropriate for your complaint. Here are the regional offices:

Region I: Serves Connecticut, Maine, Massachusetts, New Hampshire, Rhode Island and Vermont

Secretarial Representative
U.S. Dept. of Transportation
Transportation Systems Center
55 Broadway
Cambridge, Massachusetts 02142

Region II: Serves New York, New Jersey, Puerto Rico and Virgin Islands

Secretarial Representative
U.S. Dept. of Transportation
26 Federal Plaza, Room 1811
New York, New York 10007

Region III: Serves Delaware, District of Columbia, Maryland, Pennsylvania, Virginia and West Virginia

Secretarial Representative
U.S. Dept. of Transportation
Mall Building, Suite 1214
325 Chestnut Street
Philadelphia, Pennsylvania 19106

Region IV: Serves Alabama, Florida, Georgia, Kentucky, Mississippi, North Carolina, South Carolina and Tennessee

Secretarial Representative
U.S. Dept. of Transportation
1720 Peachtree Road, N.W.
Suite 515
Atlanta, Georgia 30309

Region V: Serves Illinois, Indiana, Minnesota, Michigan, Ohio and Wisconsin

Secretarial Representative
U.S. Dept. of Transportation
300 South Wacker Drive
17th Floor
Chicago, Illinois 60606

Region VI: Serves Arkansas, Louisiana, New Mexico, Oklahoma and Texas

Secretarial Representative
U.S. Dept. of Transportation
9-C-18 Federal Center
1100 Commerce Street
Dallas, Texas 75202

Region VII: Serves Iowa, Kansas, Missouri and Nebraska

Secretarial Representative
U.S. Dept. of Transportation
601 East 12th Street
Room 634
Kansas City, Missouri 64106

Region VIII: Serves Colorado, Montana, North Dakota, South Dakota, Utah and Wyoming

Secretarial Representative
U.S. Dept. of Transportation
Prudential Plaza, Suite 1822
1050 17th Street
Denver, Colorado 80202

Region IX: Serves Arizona, California, Hawaii, Nevada and Guam

Secretarial Representative
U.S. Dept. of Transportation
450 Golden Gate Avenue
Box 36133
San Francisco, California 94102

Region X: Serves Alaska, Idaho, Oregon and Washington

Secretarial Representative
U.S. Dept. of Transportation
1321 Second Avenue, Room 5079
Seattle, Washington 98101

ENVIRONMENTAL PROTECTION AGENCY

The EPA is concerned with pollution of all kinds: of air or water, from noise, oil spills, or contamination resulting from any use of industrial or agricultural chemicals. Thus, the EPA is responsible for many regulations, from emission-control devices on your car to halting the building of a new hydro-electric plant that threatens life in a river. If you have a complaint that involves problems of this character, especially if they clearly involve traffic across state lines, contact the regional office of the EPA. In some cases, you should contact your state or local EPA first, but these agencies are often concerned with more localized issues, such as garbage disposal.

Region I: Serves Connecticut, Maine, Massachusetts, New Hampshire, Rhode Island and Vermont

EPA Region I
J. F. K. Building
Boston, Massachusetts 02203
(617) 223-7210

Region II: Serves New Jersey, New
             York, Puerto Rico and
             Virgin Islands

EPA Region II
26 Federal Plaza
New York, New York 10007
(212) 264-2525

Region III: Serves Delaware, Mary-
             land, Pennsylvania,
             Virginia, West Virginia
             and District of Columbia

EPA Region III
6th and Walnut Streets
Philadelphia, Pennsylvania 19106
(215) 597-5727

Region IV: Serves Alabama, Florida,
             Georgia, Kentucky,
             Mississippi, North Caro-
             lina, South Carolina and
             Tennessee

EPA Region IV
1421 Peachtree Street, N.E.
Atlanta, Georgia 30309
(404) 526-5727

Region V: Serves Illinois, Indiana,
             Michigan, Minnesota, Ohio
             and Wisconsin

EPA Region V
230 South Dearborn Street
Chicago, Illinois 60604
(312) 353-5250

Region VI: Serves Arkansas, Louisi-
             ana, New Mexico, Oklahoma
             and Texas

EPA Region VI
1600 Patterson Street
Dallas, Texas 75201
(214) 749-1962

Region VII: Serves Iowa, Kansas,
             Missouri and Nebraska

EPA Region VII
1735 Baltimore Avenue
Kansas City, Missouri 64108
(816) 374-3895

Region VIII: Serves Colorado, Mon-
             tana, North Dakota,
             South Dakota, Utah and
             Wyoming

EPA Region VIII
1860 Lincoln Street
Denver, Colorado 80203
(303) 837-3895

Region IX: Serves Arizona, Califor-
             nia, Hawaii, Nevada,
             American Samoa, Guam,
             Trust Territories of the
             Pacific and Wake Island

EPA Region IX
100 California Street
San Francisco, California 94111
(415) 556-2320

Region X: Serves Alaska, Idaho, Ore-
             gon and Washington

EPA Region X
1200 Sixth Avenue
Seattle, Washington 98101
(206) 442-1220

FEDERAL AVIATION ADMINISTRATION

While the Civil Aeronautics Board regulates air carriers to achieve free and fair commercial competition, it is the responsibility of the FAA to regulate for air safety. Everything from air traffic patterns over crowded airports to screening passengers for concealed weapons before a flight is supervised by the FAA. The place to contact, whether you are pilot or air traveler, is the

>Community and Consumer Liaison Division
>AIS 400
>Federal Aviation Administration
>800 Independence Avenue, S.W.
>Washington, D. C. 20591

If you have a suggestion or complaint about something going on in a particular area, write one of the regional offices listed below:

Eastern Region:	Serves New York, New Jersey, Pennsylvania, Delaware, Maryland, West Virginia and Virginia	Federal Building J.F.K. International Airport Jamaica, New York 11430
Central Region:	Serves Nebraska, Iowa, Kansas and Missouri	601 East 12th Street Kansas City, Missouri 64101
Great Lakes Region:	Serves Minnesota, Wisconsin, Michigan, Illinois, Indiana and Ohio	2300 East Devon Avenue Des Plaines, Illinois 60018
New England Region:	Serves Maine, Vermont, New Hampshire, Massachusetts, Connecticut and Rhode Island	12 New England Executive Park Burlington, Massachusetts 08103

Northwest Region: Serves Washington, Oregon and Idaho

FAA Building
King County International Airport
Seattle, Washington 98108

Rocky Mountain Region: Serves Montana, North Dakota, South Dakota, Wyoming, Utah and Colorado

P. O. Box 7213
Denver, Colorado 80207

Southern Region: Serves Kentucky, Tennessee, North Carolina, South Carolina, Mississippi, Alabama, Georgia, Florida and Puerto Rico

P. O. Box 20636
Atlanta, Georgia 30320

Southwest Region: Serves New Mexico, Oklahoma, Texas, Arkansas and Louisiana

P. O. Box 1689
Fort Worth, Texas 76101

Western Region: Serves Arizona, California and Nevada

P. O. Box 92007
Worldway Postal Center
Los Angeles, California 90019

Alaskan Region: Serves Alaska

632 6th Avenue
Anchorage, Alaska 99501

Pacific-Asia Region: Serves this entire area

P. O. Box 4009
Honolulu, Hawaii 96812

FEDERAL COMMUNICATIONS COMMISSION

The FCC licenses all radio and television stations in their use of the public air. If any licensee does not use that air in the public interest, he can have his license taken away or suspended by the FCC. Complaints by listeners or viewers often result in new regulations or relaxation of old ones, though few stations actually are put off the air by the FCC. When a new station comes into being, however, license hearings are often very tough, and consumer comment, for or against, can make all the difference. If you want to complain about the practices and policies of any broadcast station or to comment on any potential station, simply write to the

>	Secretary of the FCC
>	Washington, D. C. 20554.

Your complaint might be about commercials, program content, lack of public interest programming, failure to abide by the equal time provision, inappropriate language, or anything else you see or hear that seems to you to be distinctly against the public interest.

FEDERAL ENERGY ADMINISTRATION

Important-sounding as this agency seems, especially in our energy-short times, the FEA is more of a study group and referral agency than an active one. The time is probably not far off when the United States will have a cabinet-level energy department, with the same kind of clout as the Department of the Interior or the Department of Agriculture. If you do have a consumer problem in the area of energy, the FEA will be able to refer you to an agency more directly able to help. Write the

>	Office of Consumer Affairs/Special Impact
>	Federal Energy Administration
>	Room 4310, Federal Building
>	Washington, D. C. 20461

FEDERAL TRADE COMMISSION

The FTC, like the CAB and many of our older consumer-oriented agencies, is charged with protecting the public against practices that unfairly limit or restrain competition. Among these are price-fixing, deceptive advertising, bait-and-switch practices, and dozens of others. The FTC issues yearly guidelines to business and industry, and will also give quasi-legal advice to businesses and individuals who ask for it. If you, as a businessperson, have any doubt about the legality of a practice, the FTC is the place to turn for advice. And if you have a consumer complaint that has not been attended by the business in question or local agencies, you may want to get in touch with the regional office of the FTC.

Some things to consider before writing or calling the Federal Trade Commission: Does your complaint involve interstate commerce? Remember, this is a federal agency. Is yours a problem of more than individual interest? The FTC isn't likely to intervene if you and a merchant have a dispute over a malfunctioning toaster. But if the question is one of wide-spread business practices that you consider unfair, the FTC might very well be interested. The Commission itself can't throw a merchant in jail or levy a fine, but it can take the matter to court if the authority of the FTC alone isn't enough to stop the disputed practices.

REGIONAL OFFICES

Atlanta

730 Peachtree Street, N.E.
Room 800
Atlanta, Georgia 30308
(404) 526-5836

Boston

1301 Analex Building
150 Causeway
Boston, Massachusetts 12114
(617) 223-6621

Chicago

55 East Monroe Street-Suite 1437
Chicago, Illinois 60603
(312) 352-4423

Cleveland

Federal Office Building, Room 1339
1240 East 9th Street
Cleveland, Ohio 44199
(216) 522-4307

Dallas

500 South Ervay Street, Room 452-B
Dallas, Texas 75201
(214) 749-3056

Denver

128 U. S. Customs House
721 19th Street
Denver, Colorado 80202
(303) 837-2871

Los Angeles

11000 Wilshire Boulevard, Room 13209
Los Angeles, California 90024
(213) 824-7575

New York

26 Federal Plaza
Federal Building, 22nd Floor
New York, New York 10007
(212) 264-1270

San Francisco

450 Golden Gate Avenue, Box 36005
San Francisco, California 94102
(415) 556-1270

Seattle

28th Floor, Federal Building
Seattle, Washington 98174
(206) 442-4655

Washington, D. C.

Gelman Building
2120 L Street, N.W.
Washington, D. C. 20037
(202) 254-7700

For consumer information, write the

> Bureau of Consumer Protection
> Federal Trade Commission
> 6th Street and Pennsylvania Avenue, N.W.
> Washington, D. C. 20580

FOOD AND DRUG ADMINISTRATION

Complaints concerning product mislabeling, unsanitary packaging, and misleading claims for food, drug, cosmetic or medical devices fall under the jurisdiction of the FDA. If you think such a product was harmful or potentially harmful to you, the FDA is the place to go. You should state clearly everything that happened, and also provide brand name, store where the device or product was purchased, and any code number that may appear on the label. If possible, retain the unused portion for possible laboratory examination. Address complaints to the national office of the

>Food and Drug Administration
>5600 Fishers Lane
>Rockville, Maryland 20852
>(301) 433-3380

In most cases, you should start by reporting complaints first to the regional offices as listed below:

<u>Atlanta</u>

880 West Peachtree Street, N.W.
Atlanta, Georgia 30309
(404) 526-5265 and 3162

<u>Tampa</u>

Tampa, Florida 33607
(813) 228-7494

<u>Baltimore</u>

900 Madison Avenue
Baltimore, Maryland 21201
(301) 962-3396 and 3397

<u>Falls Church</u>

Falls Church, Virginia 22046
(703) 557-0389

<u>Boston</u>

585 Commercial Street
Boston, Massachusetts 02109
(617) 223-3171

<u>Albany</u>

Albany, New York 12207
(518) 472-6045

<u>Chicago</u>

Main Post Office Building, Room 1222
433 West Van Buren Street
Chicago, Illinois 60607
(312) 353-7126

<u>Cincinnati</u>

1141 Central Parkway
Cincinnati, Ohio 45202
(513) 584-3500

<u>Cleveland</u>

Cleveland, Ohio 44114
(216) 522-4802

<u>Dallas</u>

500 South Ervay, Suite 490-B
Dallas, Texas 75201
(214) 749-2383 and 2384

<u>Denver</u>

New Customhouse Bldg., Room 500
20th and California Streets
Denver, Colorado 80202
(303) 827-4917

<u>Detroit</u>

1560 East Jefferson Avenue
Detroit, Michigan 48207
(313) 226-6260

<u>Indianapolis</u>

Indianapolis, Indiana 46204
(317) 633-5730

<u>Kansas City</u>

1000 Cherry Street
Kansas City, Missouri 64106
(816) 374-5623

St. Louis

St. Louis, Missouri 63101
(314) 622-4137

Los Angeles

1521 West Pico Boulevard
Los Angeles, California 90015
(213) 688-3771

Minneapolis

240 Hennepin Avenue
Minneapolis, Minnesota 55401
(612) 725-2121

Seattle

Federal Office Building
Room 5003, 909 First Avenue
Seattle, Washington 98104
(206) 442-5258

New Orleans

U. S. Customhouse, Room 222
423 Canal Street
New Orleans, Louisiana 70130
(504) 527-2420 and 2401

New York

850 Third Avenue
Brooklyn, New York 11232
(212) 788-5000, Ext. 1265

Newark

970 Broad Street, Room 831
Newark, New Jersey 07102
(201) 645-3265

Philadelphia

U.S. Customhouse, Room 1204
2nd and Chestnut Streets
Philadelphia, Pennsylvania 19106
(215) 597-4374 and 0387

San Francisco

Federal Office Building
50 Fulton Street, Room 544
San Francisco, California 94102
(415) 556-2062 and 7672

San Juan

P. O. Box 4427
Old San Juan Station
San Juan, Puerto Rico 00905
(809) 723-6130

INTERSTATE COMMERCE COMMISSION

The ICC regulates passenger and freight transportation across state lines. This includes busses, trains and trucking. All interstate carriers are required to file a bond with the ICC against accidental loss, damage, injury or death. If you have a complaint concerning any interstate transportation, whether of people, household goods, or merchandise, report it to the

Interstate Commerce Commission
Washington, D. C. 20423

There is a toll-free hotline for inquiries: (800) 424-9312.

NATIONAL BUREAU OF STANDARDS

The Office of Weights and Measures of the National Bureau of Standards regulates almost every weight and measure involved in business. It is the job of this office to see that a package marked "1 quart" or "1 liter" really contains the amount stated. If you think you have a problem related to short weights or inadequate measures, the first thing to do is see if your locality has a weights or standards listing. But if it doesn't, or if for some reason they can't help you, direct your complaint to the

>National Conference on Weights and Measures
>National Bureau of Standards
>Washington, D. C. 20234
>(301) 921-3677

NATIONAL HIGHWAY TRAFFIC SAFETY ADMINISTRATION

If you think your vehicle, or the vehicle you rode on, is unsafe at any speed, and you think this is a fault of the manufacturer, seller, or importer, then you have a complaint of the kind that interests the NHTSA. This office sets the safety standards that all new cars, buses, trucks, trailers, recreational vehicles and motorcycles have to meet. It is the NHTSA that compels a manufacturer from time to time to recall automobiles to correct a structural defect that has caused or might cause accidents. There are substantial penalties under law for non-compliance with this agency. If you think you know of a safety defect in your car or in a commercial vehicle, write the

>Office of Consumer Affairs
>National Highway Traffic Safety Administration
>400 Seventh Street, S.W.
>Washington, D. C. 20590
>(202) 426-0670

OFFICE OF CONSUMER AFFAIRS

The Office of Consumer Affairs, a division of the Department of Health, Education, and Welfare (HEW), is pretty much an advocate to the President and the Congress on behalf of the consumer. Although they receive many specific complaints from consumers, the OCA isn't empowered to do anything about them other than use the complaints and suggestions of consumers to promote effective legislation and policies within the Executive Branch. There are many useful consumer-education publications available from the OCA, as well as certain liaison functions. For more information, contact the

>   Executive Secretariat
>   Office of Consumer Affairs
>   Department of Health, Education and Welfare
>   Independence and 4th Street, S.W.
>   Washington, D. C. 20201
>   (202) 245-6093

SECURITIES AND EXCHANGE COMMISSION

The SEC regulates the sale of stocks and bonds to prevent fraud or misleading practices in the securities market. It handles complaints about the stock market, investment brokers and advisers, and the National Association of Securities Dealers. Public companies must file reports with the SEC, and these are available to the public in Washington, D. C. If you want to inquire about these reports, or any other aspect of securities sale, contact a regional office of the SEC. The national headquarters address is:

>   Securities and Exchange Commission
>   Washington, D. C. 20549

U. S. POSTAL SERVICE

Postal employees, for the most part, are unusually dedicated, hard-working types who are inclined to give the extra push that service difficulties require. Because of this, you are usually better off taking your complaint or difficulty down to the post office to engage the personal attention of one of the people working there. The farther you get from the "scene of the crime," the less likely anybody is to know what you're talking about. On occasion, however, you run into a stone wall instead of a smiling face. Or maybe you run into both. If it happens to you, be advised that there is a higher authority, and that it will pay attention. Ask your post office for a Consumer Service Card. This is the official complaint form, and it ensures that Washington will be watching to see how your problem is solved. If that doesn't work, write directly to the

        Consumer Advocate
        The U. S. Postal Service
        Washington, D. C. 20260

Chapter 8: TRADE ASSOCIATIONS

Like the little girl in the old nursery rhyme, when Trade Associations are good, they are very, very good. Better, in fact, than government agencies, however well-intentioned. Unfortunately, this directory cannot tell you for sure which trade and industry groups are strong for the consumer at the moment. First, you'll always have your best luck with a local office, and these change in their effectiveness with changing times and personnel. Second, new groups are always coming into being and withering away, depending on conditions within the industry. Listed below are some of the traditionally strong national organizations. When you have a complaint or question about a specific industry, look up the name of the relevant trade association here, then look in your telephone directory to see if there's a chapter near you. If there isn't, or the local group seems spineless, then write or call the national headquarters. Make sure you've tried the local folks first, because the national chapter will just refer you back to them if you haven't.

It's a good idea to keep your eyes open for new associations, since they pop up all the time. If you see or hear of any not listed here, look up their numbers and addresses in your telephone directory, jot them down, and keep them with this list, to complete and update it. Often, the local Chamber of Commerce or Better Business Bureau will be able to tell you about new or useful industry groups.

APPAREL

American Apparel Manufacturers
  Association
1611 North Kent Street
Arlington, Virginia 22209
(703) 522-8070

American Footwear Manufacturers
  Association
1611 North Kent Street
Arlington, Virginia 22209
(703) 522-8070

American Knitwear Manufacturers
  Association
350 Fifth Avenue
New York, New York 10001
(212) 947-1250

National Shoe Retailers
200 Madison Avenue
New York, New York 10016
(212) 686-7520

BICYCLES

Bicycle Institute of America
122 East 42nd Street
New York, New York 10017
(212) 697-6340

CARS

Automatic Car Wash Association
  International
1059 Mannheim Road
P. O. Box 66
Bellwood, Illinois 60104

Automotive Parts and Accessories
  Association, Inc.
1411 K Street
Washington, D. C. 20005

Independent Garage Owners of
  America
624 South Michigan Avenue
Chicago, Illinois 60605

National Automobile Dealers
  Association
2000 K Street, N.W.
Washington, D. C. 20006

National Tire Dealers and Re-
  treaders Association, Inc.
1343 L Street, N.W.
Washington, D. C. 20005

CREDIT

Associated Credit Bureaus, Inc.
6767 Southwest Freeway
Houston, Texas 77036

Consumer Bankers Association
1725 K Street, N.W.
Washington, D. C. 20006
(202) 466-2590

International Consumer Credit
  Association
375 Jackson Avenue
St. Louis, Missouri 63130

National Consumer Finance
  Association
1000 16th Street, N.W.
Washington, D. C. 20036
(202) 638-1340

EMPLOYMENT

National Employment Association
Suite 353
2000 K Street, N.W.
Washington, D. C. 20006

FLORISTS

Society of American Florists and
  Ornamental Horticulturists
901 North Washington Street
Alexandria, Virginia 22341

FOOD

National Institute of Locker and
  Freezer Provisioners
224 East High Street
Elizabethtown, Pennsylvania 17022

FURNISHINGS

American Gas Association
1515 Wilson Boulevard
Arlington, Virginia 22209

Association of Home Appliance
  Manufacturers
20 North Wacker Drive
Chicago, Illinois 60606

Carpet and Rug Institute
Consumer Action Panel
P. O. Box 2048
Dalton, Georgia 30720
(404) 278-3176

Furniture Industry Consumer Action
  Panel
P. O. Box 951
High Point, North Carolina 27261

Major Appliance Consumer Action
  Panel
20 North Wacker Drive
Chicago, Illinois 60606
(312) 236-3165

National Alliance of Television and
  Electronic Service Association
5908 South Troy Street
Chicago, Illinois 60629
(312) 476-6363

HARDWARE

National Retail Hardware Association
964 North Pennsylvania Street
Indianapolis, Indiana 46204

HOMES

American Institute of Kitchen
  Dealers
199 Main Street
Hackettstown, New Jersey 07804

National Association of Real Estate Boards
155 East Superior Street
Chicago, Illinois 60611

National Home Improvement Council
11 East 44th Street
New York, New York 10017
(212) 867-0121

National Remodelers Association
50 East 42nd Street
New York, New York 10017
(212) 687-5224

National Society of Interior De-
  signers
315 East 62nd Street
New York, New York 10021
(212) 838-5906

Office of Interstate Land Sales
  Registration
Department of Housing and Urban
  Development
Washington, D. C. 20401
(202) 755-5860
(U. S. Government)

HOME STUDY

National Home Study Council
1601 18th Street, N.W.
Washington, D. C. 20009
(202) 234-5100

INSURANCE

National Association of Life Un-
  derwriters
1922 F Street, N.W.
Washington, D. C. 20006

National Association of Mutual
   Insurance Companies
Suite H
2611 East 46th Street
Indianapolis, Indiana 46205

LAUNDRY

American Institute of Laundering
Joliet, Illinois 60434
(815) 727-4501

International Fabricare Institute
Chicago Street and Doris Avenue
Joliet, Illinois 60433
(815) 727-4501

National Institute of Drycleaning
909 Burlington Avenue
Silver Spring, Maryland 20910

LAWYERS

American Bar Association
1705 De Sales Street, N.W.
Washington, D. C. 20036
(202) 659-1330

MAIL

Direct Mail/Marketing Association, Inc.
Consumer Relations Department
6 East 43rd Street
New York, New York 10017

Director Selling Association
1730 M Street, N.W., Suite 610
Washington, D. C. 20036

Mail Order Action Line
Direct Mail Advertising Association
230 Park Avenue
New York, New York 10017
(212) 689-4977

MOBILE HOMES

Mobile Homes Manufacturers As-
   sociation
P. O. Box 35
Chantilly, Virginia 22021

Mobile Homes Consumer Affairs
   Council
P. O. Box 3163
Anaheim, California 92803
(Western States Only)

Southeastern Mobile Housing Institute
348 East Paces Ferry Road, N.E.
Atlanta, Georgia 30305
(Southeastern States Only)

MEDICAL

American Dental Association
211 East Chicago Avenue
Chicago, Illinois 60611

American Medical Association
1776 K Street, N.W.
Washington, D. C. 20006
(202) 833-8310

Better Hearing Institute
1001 Connecticut Avenue, N.W.
Washington, D. C. 20036
(800) 424-8576 free

National Hearing Aid Society
24261 Grand River
Detroit, Michigan 48219

Optical Manufacturers Association
30 East 42nd Street
New York, New York 10017

Pharmaceutical Manufacturers Association
1155 15th Street, N.W.
Washington, D. C. 20005

PHOTOGRAPHY

Master Photo Dealers and Finishers Association
603 Lansing Avenue
Jackson, Michigan 49202

Photo Marketing Association
Consumer Affairs Department
603 Lansing Avenue
Jackson, Michigan 49202
(517) 783-2807

ROOFING AND REPAIRS

National Roofing Contractors Association
1515 Harlem Avenue
Oak Park, Illinois 60302
(312) 383-6032

Sheet Metal and Air Conditioning Contractors
National Association
1611 North Kent Street
Arlington, Virginia 22209

TRAVEL

American Hotel and Motel Association
888 Seventh Avenue
New York, New York 10019
(212) 265-4056

American Society of Travel Agents
360 Lexington Avenue
New York, New York 10019
(212) 661-2424

National Restaurant Association
1530 Lake Shore Drive
Chicago, Illinois 60610

TOYS

Toy Manufacturers of America
200 Fifth Avenue
New York, New York 10010
(212) 675-1141

WATCHES AND JEWELRY

Jewelers Vigilance Committee, Inc.
919 Third Avenue
New York, New York 10022
(212) 753-1304

Watchmakers of Switzerland Information Center, Inc.
608 Fifth Avenue
New York, New York 10020
(212) 757-7030

Watchmakers of Switzerland Information Center, Inc.
606 South Hill Street
Los Angeles, California 90014
(213) 627-2636

Chapter 9: SMALL CLAIMS COURT

According to some estimates, 80% of all consumer complaints involve amounts under $250.00. This is under the maximum allowed for disputes in Small Claims Courts in most states. Unlike Civil Court, Small Claims Court need not cost you a lot in legal fees or court costs. You don't have to have a lawyer at all to file or win a small claims suit, and in many areas, lawyers are discouraged from participating in such suits. Since you can argue your own case, you'll have to take the time to bone up on the rules (help is available from the Clerk of the Small Claims Court) and to prepare your case. If you qualify, you can also get advice from a Legal Aid lawyer.

Small Claims Courts, whether or not lawyers are permitted, are designed to let citizens plead their own cases, in ordinary language. You will not have to learn legal jargon or the complex ins and outs of obscure statutes in order to win. The atmosphere is purposely relaxed, and officials of the court will give you all the help they can, before and during the hearing. But this doesn't mean that you should stroll into court unprepared and expect to win. Although the preparation is common-sense rather than legalistic, you must study and observe the rules for the Small Claims Court in your area. The time you spend in researching and preparing is not allowable as part of your claim. If your time is worth more than your claim, you may want to consider a civil suit, or some other way of resolving the matter.

If you do decide that Small Claims Court may be the answer, get the information for your area right away. The upper limits of small claims vary from state to state, as do the fees for filing a suit. Check your telephone directory for an up-to-date listing of the relevant phone number. Since numbers and locations change without warning, this year's phone book is the most reliable source, but see also the directory provided in this chapter. If you don't find a listing under Small Claims Court, try Justice of the Peace Court, or Magistrate's Court, or call the Civil Court and ask for information.

Important points to ask about are: 1. What is the upper limit for claims in this court? 2. What is the filing fee? (Approximate limits and fees are provided here, but costs for Small Claims Court, like everything else these days, tend to shoot up at a moment's notice.) 3. Does the clerk have any written rules or guidelines that he or she can send you? 4. Are lawyers permitted? If so, what may they do? (Even if you don't want a lawyer, you should know if your opponent may bring one or not.)

If you've decided to try Small Claims, you'll start to prepare. Before you issue any summonses or other challenges, be sure you have done all you can to settle the matter without going to court. You'll have to present evidence of such attempts to the judge or arbitrator who hears your case, so assemble all your documentation right at the beginning. Many small claims are settled at the outset, when the complainant realizes that perhaps he has not given his adversary sufficient notice of his demands. But if you have made four phone calls and written six letters, all without getting a satisfactory response, this avenue is probably exhausted. Assemble all the carbon copies of the letters, write down times and dates of calls or interviews, and, just to be sure, send the offending party a letter stating that you plan to take him to Small Claims if he does not respond within two days.

Determine your eligibility for making a small claim by making up your mind how much you want to recover. Remember, you cannot ask for the full purchase price of a defective item, even if you've only used it one day. You might decide to ask for the amount it would take to have the product repaired, however. If your estimate of what is coming to you is far over the limit of the court, you'll either want to hire a lawyer and go into regular Civil Court, or search out a new avenue of approach.

Once you've determined to go ahead, it's time to pay the filing fees and costs for serving whatever summonses and subpoenas you and the clerk decide are necessary. Lots of help is available to you at this point, from clerks and other officials of the court. It's best to make a trip to the office, rather than trying to handle such things by mail or over the phone. You'll be told, for example, that you must find out the exact legal corporate name of the firm you want to sue. This name, even if the company never uses it, is on file with the secretary of state in your state.

After you have issued your summons and/or subpoena, you may hear from that crusty old type down at Acme Used Cars who was always too busy to talk to you before. If you do, listen to what he has to say. It is almost always better to settle out of Small Claims Court than in it. First, the judge will look with disfavor on any evidence that you, the complaining party, have refused reasonable offers to settle. Second, Small Claims Courts often give plaintiffs only a part of what they ask for, anyway, so you may lose nothing and gain time and money by making your own compromise and dropping the suit. You are not obliged, however, to accept terms unfavorable to you, just because a compromise is offered. If you feel you're right, go ahead.

ASSEMBLING EVIDENCE

Once you're sure that you and your adversary cannot settle the matter between you, it's time to marshall your evidence. The strongest evidence is physical proof. This can include the defective merchandise, within reason. You will not be well received if you try to bring a sick elephant or a motorcycle that leaks oil into the courtroom. Other physical evidence you should have includes receipts, contracts, written guarantees, pictures of the merchandise if it is unsuitable for direct presentation, and the evidence that you have attempted with honest good will to settle the matter out of court.

Second to physical evidence is the testimony of witnesses who are unbiased or of experts. It's always best if such people will show up to testify in person, of course, but you can bring written statements instead. It is a good idea to get written statements notarized at a bank or currency exchange. Impartial testimony aside, you should also solicit the testimony of those who are biased in your favor, such as your friends and family. Finally, you will tell your own story yourself. You and all your witnesses should remember that it is not only unnecessary to act like lawyers, it is undesirable. If the judge thinks you are well-versed in legal matters, he will tend to judge any slips very harshly. Courtroom theatrics are likewise out of place. Instruct all your witnesses to be clear and concise in their statements, getting quickly to the point and stopping as soon as the essential facts have been stated. It's a good idea to make a few notes, but not to write out a whole speech ahead of time. You and your witnesses should also be prepared to be cross-examined by the other side. Imagine any arguments they may have against your position, and think of the counter arguments.

Just at the point when you're all ready to go, your opponent may try delaying tactics. He may move for a continuance, claiming that he hasn't had enough time to prepare, or he may not show up at all. In Small Claims Court, he will probably be given the continuance, and he will probably get another chance to come to court, even if he fails to show up the first time. If this happens once to you, try to prevent it a second time by sending your opponent a telegram or registered letter a few days before the trial, reminding him of the date. You can present this to the judge as evidence if there is any more stalling. In some states, parties to a suit are given the choice of appearing before an arbitrator instead of a judge. If your adversary wants to go this route and you are fairly confident of the justice of your claim (as you should be) you may do just as well with an arbitrator. Arbitration is binding, however, which means there can be no appeal. If you think the facts are very complex and might be misunderstood the first time around, better go with the judge.

During the actual trial or hearing, you should have no trouble in your presentation if your preparation has been thorough. Just stick clearly and simply to the facts. When the defendant makes his presentation, pay close attention to whatever he says, no matter how unfair you think it is, and make notes just like the ones you made for your own presentation. You'll get your chance to bring out points when you cross-examine him. The best cross-examination is to force the other party to square his assertions with the documentation you have brought in. It will never help your case if you call your opponent a liar or engage with him in a shouting match. If the judge has any questions, answer them with the same polite, calm manner that you have used throughout. It depends on the judge whether you get your decision the same day, or a notice in the mail. However it goes, keep your composure.

Suppose you win, then what? Part of the problem with small claims is that the court will not enforce its order. You are responsible for collecting the amount owed to you. If one or two polite letters and perhaps one or two that threaten sheriff's action do not have the desired results, you may have to contact a collector. The sheriff, if there is one, must collect your debt as part of his job. He may be so busy, however, that your claim goes to the bottom of a virtually bottomless pile. A marshal can also be employed -- for a percentage of the claim -- to collect your judgment. If you can afford to wait, time is on your side. There is practically no limit to the time over which you can keep trying to collect on a Small Claims judgment.

If you lose in Small Claims Court, some states permit appeal. It's up to you, at this point, whether it's worth your time and money to pursue the matter any further. It is at this point that many consumers resort to unconventional action, such as organizing a boycott of the merchant in question. If you decide to go this route, be sure to keep your actions within the law. In a few cases, consumers consider the case so important that they decide to up the price tag and hire a lawyer for a civil suit. Since litigation often enrages people who weren't very mad to begin with, be sure you consider this and every further step in a consumer battle with as much cool reason as you can muster.

DIRECTORY OF SMALL CLAIMS COURTS

Note: The limits and fees listed here are meant only as an approximate guide. In some cases, exact figures may have changed, usually upward. Please consult the Clerk of the Court in your area for exact information.

<u>Alaska</u>: Small Claims Court

Limit: $1,000

Fees: $5 plus $10 for personal service of documents, or current rate for registered mail.
Corporations must be represented by an attorney.
Appeals allowed if filed within thirty days where claim is over $50.

<u>Alabama</u>: Justice Court

Limit: $300

Fees: $10 plus fees for service.
Appeals allowed if filed within five days, subject to new filing fee and the posting of a bond for double the amount

of judgment sought.

Arizona: Justice of the Peace or Superior Court

Limit: Justice of the Peace -- $500. Superior Court -- suits between $200 and $500.

Fees: $1 for suits under $50. $3 plus service for suits over $50.

Corporations must be represented by an attorney.

Appeals allowed to Superior Court for claims larger than $20. Must be filed within five days. Fees: $24 plus posting of a bond for double the judgment sought.

Arkansas: Justice of the Peace, Mayor's or Municipal Courts

Limits: Justice of the Peace -- $200 in contract cases and actions to regain an object; $100 in personal injury cases. Municipal Courts -- $500.

Fees: $3.50.

Attorneys are preferred in Municipal Courts. Appeals allowed.

California: Small Claims Court

Limit: $500

Fees: $2 plus service.

Attorneys are not permitted.

Defendant may appeal within thirty days and must post a bond for amount of judgment sought plus $25.

Colorado: Small Claims Court

Limit: $500

Fees: $7 filing fee.

Corporations must be represented by an attorney.

Appeals by defendants allowed within five days. Appeals by plaintiff allowed in cases involving wages or labor performed.

Connecticut: Small Claims Court
Limit: $750
Fees: $3 filing fee plus $5 for service.
Appeals not allowed.
Winner must reimburse loser for filing costs, plus up to $25 for additional expenses.

Delaware: Small Claims Court or Justice of the Peace
Limit: $1,500
Fees: $10.
Appeals allowed to Superior Court within fifteen days; loser must post a bond equal to the amount of judgment.

District of Columbia: Small Claims Court
Limit: $750
Fees: $1 plus fees for service
Appeals allowed within three days; application is made to Court Clerk.

Florida: Small Claims cases heard by the County Courts.

Georgia: Small Claims Court
Limit: Varies throughout the state.
Fees: Vary.
Corporations may not bring suit in Atlanta, but may in others.
Appeals allowed only in Atlanta.

Hawaii: Small Claims Court
Limit: $300
Fee: $3 plus fees for service; fees waived if plaintiff is unable to pay.
Appeals not allowed.

Idaho: Small Claims Court
Limit: $200
Fees: $5 plus fees for service.
Attorneys are not permitted.
Appeals are allowed within thirty days with posting of bond.
Losers must pay $25 expenses to winners.

Illinois: Small Claims Court
Limit: $1,000
Fees: $7 for cases less than $500; $10 for cases above $500, plus fees for service.
Corporations must be represented by attorneys.
Appeals allowed within thirty days, or within five days for cases involving rents.
Defendant may request a jury trial at a cost of $25 for a twelve-person jury or $12.50 for a six-person jury.

Indiana: Justice of the Peace
Limit: $500
Fees: $6.
Corporations must be represented by attorneys.
Appeals allowed to Circuit or Superior Court within thirty days; appeal period may be extended.

Iowa: Justice of the Peace or Conciliation Court

Limit: $100, or $300 if both parties consent; Conciliation Courts are used for cases of less than $100 which would otherwise go to District Court.

Fees: $9.

Attorneys are allowed in Justice of the Peace Court, but not in Conciliation Court.

District Court Conciliations offer the choice of arbitration.

Kansas: Conciliation Court

Limit: $100

Fees: $10.

Arbitration is available after a hearing in Conciliation Court without attorneys.

Appeals are allowed to a District Court in cases involving more than $50.

Kentucky: Justice of the Peace

Limit: Justice of the Peace -- $50. Claims between $50 and $500 may be filed either in Justice's Court or regular courts.

Fees: Vary with location and size of claim.

Appeals are not allowed, but new trials may be sought.

Louisiana: City Court or Justice of the Peace

Limit: $100 in Justice's Courts; $500 in City Courts; in New Orleans, claims between $100 and $500 may be brought in City Court or in District Court.

Fees: $10.

Appeals are allowed only on points of law.

Maine: Small Claims Court

Limit: $200

Fees: $5.

      Appeals are allowed on points of law.

Maryland: Small Claims Court

Limit: $1,000

Fees: $5 for claims up to $500; $10 for larger claims.

      Appeals are allowed if filed within thirty days.

Massachusetts: Small Claims Court

Limit: $400

Fees: Vary with locality, with a maximum of $3.

      Appeals are not allowed.

Michigan: Small Claims Court

Limit: From $300 to $500, depending on the locality.

Fees: Vary with the locality.

      Appeals are allowed to Circuit Court.

Minnesota: Conciliation Court

Limit: $300, except $500 in the Twin Cities and Duluth.

Fees: $3.

      Attorneys are not permitted.

      Arbitration is available.

      Appeals are allowed to Municipal Court within ten days; bond, additional fees, and an affidavit must also be filed.

Mississippi: Justice of the Peace
Limit: $200
Fees: $6.
> Appeals are allowed within ten days; bond must be posted for double the judgment sought, with a minimum of $100. Defendant or plaintiff may request a trial with a six-person jury.

Missouri: Magistrate's Court
Limit: From $2,000 to $3,500.
Fees: $9.
> Appeals are not allowed, but a new trial may be requested in the Circuit Court.

Montana: Justice's Court
Limit: $300
Fees: $2.50, or nothing, if you can show yourself impoverished.
> Appeals are allowed to District Court within thirty days plus posting of a bond for double the amount of judgment sought or cash deposit of $300 over the amount of judgment sought.
>
> Either party may request a jury trial.

Nebraska: Small Claims Court or Justice of the Peace
Limit: $200 for Justice of the Peace; $500 for Small Claims Court.
Fees: $4 for Small Claims Court.
> Attorneys are not permitted in Small Claims Court.
>
> Appeals of Justice's rulings are allowed to District Court within ten days if a bond is posted for twice the amount of

judgment sought; appeals of Small Claims Court judgments can be made to Municipal Court.

Nevada: Small Claims Court
Limit: $300
Fees: $5.

Appeals are allowed to District Court within five days; a bond for twice the amount of judgment sought plus $15 must be posted.

New Hampshire: Small Claims Court
Limit: $300
Fees: $1.50 plus fees for service.

Appeals are allowed to the New Hampshire Supreme Court only on points of law.

New Jersey: Small Claims Court
Limit: $200, except in cases involving security deposits, where the limit is $50.
Fees: $2.10, plus $.40 for each additional defendant.

Appeals are allowed.

New Mexico: Small Claims Court
Limit: $2,000 for counties with populations over 100,000.
Fees: $6.50 plus fees for service.

Appeals are allowed to District Court within thirty days; bond must be posted.

New York: Small Claims Court
Limit: $500

Fees: $2 plus postage.

Corporations must be represented by an attorney.

Voluntary arbitration is available.

Appeals are allowed where "substantial injustice" can be demonstrated.

Jury trial is available on request from the defendant if he or she swears that there are issues of fact requiring a jury trial and posts a $50 bond.

North Carolina: Small Claims Court
Limit: $300
Fees: $7 for cases of less than $100; $10 if more than $100, plus $2 for each additional defendant.

Appeals for a new trial are allowed to District Court if filed within ten days of the old trial; appellant must file a surety bond.

North Dakota: Small Claims Court
Limit: $200
Fees: $2 plus $1 for each additional defendant.

Appeals are allowed to District Court if filed within ten days. Either party may request a six-person jury.

Ohio: Small Claims Court
Limit: $150
Fees: $2 plus postage.

Voluntary conciliation is available.

Corporations must have an attorney to argue in the Court, although they may simply appear without a lawyer.

Plaintiff may request a jury trial.

No appeal is allowed except in cases of trial by jury.

<u>Oklahoma</u>: Small Claims Court

Limit: $400

Fees: $3; $10 in personal property cases.

Counterclaim, if any, by defendant must be filed forty-eight hours before the trial and must be served on plaintiff; either party to the dispute may request a court reporter or jury forty-eight hours before trial after making a deposit of $25.

Appeals are allowed to the State Supreme Court within thirty days; bond is required; collection agents or assignees may not appeal.

<u>Oregon</u>: Small Claims Court or District Court

Limit: $20 for Small Claims Court; $20 to $500 in either Small Claims Court or District Court.

Fees: $1 if less than $20; $2 if $20-$100; $3 if $100-$200; $4 if $200-$300; $5 if $300-$400; $6 if $400-$500; defendant is required to pay $1.

Attorneys are allowed by consent of the presiding judge. Corporations may be represented by a lawyer only to argue for transfer of the case from Small Claims Court to District Court.

Appeals are allowed by defendants only to Circuit Court within ten days.

<u>Pennsylvania</u>: Small Claims or Justice of the Peace

Limit: $500

Fees: Varies from place to place; in Philadelphia, $6 plus fees for service.

Corporations in Philadelphia Small Claims Courts must be represented by an attorney.

Appeals are allowed to the Court of Common Pleas.

Puerto Rico: District Court or Small Claims Court
Limit: $100 in Small Claims; $2,500 in District Court.
Fees: $1.

Appeals from Small Claims to District Court are allowed.

Rhode Island: Small Claims Court
Limit: $300
Fees: $1 plus postage.

Corporations must be represented by an attorney.

Appeals by defendant only are allowed after payment of a $50 fee plus $20 for costs.

South Carolina: Small Claims Court
Limit: $200, except in Chester County where the limit is $1,000.
Fees: Vary from county to county.

Appeals are allowed on ten days' notice.

South Dakota: Justice's Courts, Police Courts; also District or Municipal Courts
Limit: $100 in Justice's and Police Courts; $500 in others.
Fees: Generally, $2.

No appeals are allowed unless defendant requests a jury trial.

Tennessee: Justice of the Peace or Court of General Sessions

Limit: $3,000

Fees: $25 in Court of General Sessions, waived in cases of impoverishment; some Justice's Courts require a bond for costs.

Appeals are allowed within ten days.

Texas: Small Claims Court

Limit: Generally $150; $200 in cases of wages or labor performed.

Fees: $3 plus fee for service.

No entity, personal or corporate, which lends money at interest may use Small Claims Court.

Either party may request a jury trial with 24-hour notice and payment of a $3 fee.

Appeals are allowed to County Court.

Utah: Small Claims Court

Limit: $200

Fees: $3 plus fee for service.

Appeals are allowed to District Court on one-month notice and deposit for costs.

Vermont: Small Claims Court

Limit: $250

Fees: $2 if less than $100; $5 if more than $100, plus fees for service.

No appeal is allowed.

Defendant may request a jury trial after payment of a $4 fee and filing an affidavit stating cause.

Virginia: Court Not of Record or regular courts
Limit: $3,000; cases above $300 may be tried in regular court.
Fees: $3.50.
Appeals are allowed in cases involving more than $50 if appeal is made within ten days and a bond is posted.

Washington: Small Claims Court
Limit: $100, except in the more populous counties, where the limit is $200.
Fees: $1 plus fees for service.
Attorneys are not allowed in cases originating in Small Claims Court.
No appeals are allowed.

West Virginia: Justice of the Peace
Limit: $300
Fees: $5 plus $2.50 for each defendant.
Appeals are allowed in cases involving more than $15 if filed within ten days; bond must be posted for double the amount of judgment sought.

Wisconsin: Small Claims Court
Limit: $500
Fees: $4.50 plus fees for service.
Voluntary arbitration is available.
Either party may request a jury trial upon payment of a fee of $24, plus $11 surtax and $6 clerk's fee.
Appeals are allowed to Circuit Court if filed within twen-

ty days; a fee of $5 plus a $5 suit tax must be paid, plus a bond for amount of judgment and costs to stay previous judgment.

Wyoming: Justice of the Peace
Limit: $100
Fees: $1.50 plus fees for service.

Voluntary arbitration is available.

Appeals are allowed in cases involving more than $25 upon payment of all costs plus a $1.50 fee or posting of a bond for twice the cost; appeals must be made within fifteen days.

Chapter 10: MEDIA AND ACTION LINES

Most of the media will keep a close watch on who they accept advertising from, because no one wants a name for carrying misleading advertising. For this reason, the media often welcome hearing if one of their advertisers is the source of a consumer complaint. So, if you have a problem with a business, it might be helpful to contact the newspaper, magazine, radio or T.V. station that carried the ad.

Additionally, no business likes to get "bad press." Keeping this thought in mind, many local newspapers, T.V. and radio stations have "Help" or "Action" lines. These give the consumer the opportunity to publicly air his or her complaint about a specific firm or organization. "Action" lines can usually handle only a limited number of complaints, but it is well worth the try.

One of the larger programs of this type, known as <u>Call for Action</u>, is run by local T.V. and radio stations. Not only will your complaint be put on the air, but a trained volunteer will attempt to help in mediating the problem between you and the businessman. The service is free. Below is a listing of local stations nationwide that provide this service to the consumer. They are listed alphabetically according to city.

Akron - WKAR
Albany - WROW

Altoona - WFBG
Baltimore - WBAL

Birmingham - WYDE

Boston - WBZ

Buffalo - WBEN TV/Radio

Chicago - WIND

Cleveland - WERE

Denver - KLZ

Detroit - WJR

Ft. Wayne - WOWO

Huntington - WGSM

Little Rock - KARK TV

Los Angeles - KFWB

Memphis - WDIA

Miami - WCIX TV

Milwaukee - WISN

Montreal - CFCF

New Bedford - WBSM

New Haven - WELI

New York - WMCA

Oklahoma City - KWTV

Omaha - WOW

Orlando - WDBO

Peoria - WRAU TV

Philadelphia - WFIL

Phoenix - KTAR TV

Pittsburgh - KDKA

Providence - WJAR

Raleigh/Durham - WRAL TV

St. Louis - KMOX

Salt Lake City - KSL

San Diego - KGTV

Seattle - KING TV

Syracuse - WHEN

Tucson - KTKT

Utica - WTLB

Washington, D. C. - WTOP

Wheeling - WWVA

In addition to <u>Call for Action</u>, some stations provide their own version of this service. If you live in the area, you might want to get in touch with one of these stations at the following addresses:

Los Angeles - KNBC TV
Action 4
P. O. Box 4444
Burbank, California 91505

New York - WNBC TV
Action 4
Box 4000
Radio City Station
New York, New York 10019

Sacramento - KCRA TV
Call Three
310 10th Street
Sacramento, California 95814

Seattle/Tacoma - KING TV
320 Aurora Avenue, North
Seattle, Washington 98109

Many newspapers have a similar service by providing an "Action" or "Hot" line column. They try to help the consumer in any way they can, whether it's a business or an uncooperative government agency that's causing the problem. Check the following list to see if your local newspaper is one of the many that provide this helpful service for the consumer.

ALABAMA

Birmingham Post Herald
  Action Line

Decatur Daily
  Action Line

ALASKA

Anchorage Times
  Action

ARIZONA

Douglas Dispatch
  Action Line

Phoenix Gazette
  Answer Line

Tucson Citizen
  Action Please!

ARKANSAS

Newport Independent
  Ask Bat

Little Rock Gazette
  Action Line (Answer Please)

Pine Bluff Commercial
  Accent

CALIFORNIA

Brawley News
  Probe

Concord Transcript
  Rap-Up

Corining Observer
  Action Line

Costa Mesa Daily Pilot
  Action Line

Fresno Bee
  Fact Finder

Hanford Sentinel
  Question Box

Indio Daily News
  Probe

Los Angeles Herald Examiner
  Action Line-Answer Line

Oakland Tribune
  Action Line

Oroville Mercury-Register
  Action

Pasadena Star-News
  Action Line

Pomona Progress Bulletin
  Action Line

Redwood City Tribune
  Action Line

Richmond Independent
  Action Man

Salinas Californian
  Action Desk

San Diego Evening Tribune
   Action Line

San Jose Mercury News
   Action Line

Santa Ana Register
   The Trouble Shooter

Santa Monica Outlook
   Trouble Shooter

COLORADO

Colorado Springs Sun
   Action Line

Longmont Times-Call
   Action Line

Loveland Reporter-Herald
   Around the Valley

CONNECTICUT

Danbury News-Times
   Action Line

Hartford Times
   Dear George

DELAWARE

Dover Delaware State Times
   Action Line

FLORIDA

Boca Raton News
   The Helper

Clearwater Sun
   Answer Man

Cocoa Today
   Help!

Fort Meyers News Press
   Reader's Line

Gainesville Sun
   Action Line

Jacksonville Journal
   Call Box

Lakeland Ledger
   Action Line Reporter

Miami Herald-News
   Action Line

St. Petersburg Times
   Independent Action

Tallahassee Democrat
   Action Line

Tampa Tribune-Times
   Troubleshooter

GEORGIA

Athens Banner-Herald
   Action One

Gainesville Times
   Action Line

Macon News
   Action Line

Valdosta Daily Times
   Times Line

HAWAII

Honolulu Star-Bulletin
   Kokua Line

IDAHO

Boise Idaho Statesman
   Action

Lewiston Tribune
   Action Forum

Nampa Free Press
   Rap

ILLINOIS

Alton Evening Telegraph
   Mr. Answer Man

Chicago Sun-Times
  Action Line

Chicago Tribune
  Action Express

Elgin Courier-News
  Do Line

Galesburg Register-Mail
  Penny for Your Thoughts

Lawrenceville Record
  For the Record

Ottawa Times
  Times Ticker

Watseka Iroquois County Journal
  Ask Us Line

INDIANA

Bloomington Herald-Telephone
  Action Line (Hot Line)

Brazil Times
  Times Line

Elkhart Truth
  Truth Line

Huntington Herald-Press
  Monday Mini's

Indianapolis News
  Herman's Hotline

Kokomo Tribune
  Action Line

LaPorte Herald-Argus
  Action Line/Hot Line

Lebanon Reporter
  Live Wire

Marion Chronicle-Tribune
  Public Forum

South Bend Tribune
  Action Line

IOWA

Sioux City Journal
  Action

KANSAS

Kansas City Kansan
  Ask the Kansan

Manhattan Mercury
  Action Line

Wichita Eagle & Beacon
  Answer Man

KENTUCKY

Madisonville Messenger
  Hot Line

LOUISIANA

Alexandria Town Talk
  Action Line

Bogalusa News
  Hot Line

Crowley Signal
  Hot Line

Lafayette Advertiser
  Action Corner

New Orleans States-Item
  Action Line

Shreveport Journal
  Action Line

MAINE

Portland Press
  Action Line (Help!)

MARYLAND

Baltimore Sun
  Direct Line

Cumberland News/Times
  Action Line

MASSACHUSETTS

Boston Globe
  Ask the Globe

Hyde Park Tribune
  Open Ear

Southbridge News
  Action Line

MICHIGAN

Ann Arbor News
  Action Please!

Detroit Free Press
  Action Line

Fenton Independent
  Hot Stuff

Greenville News
  Do Line

Jackson Citizen Patriot
  Action

Pontiac Oakland Press
  Oakland Hot Line

Ypsilanti Press
  Community Action

MINNESOTA

Duluth Budgeteer
  Action

St. Paul Pioneer Press
  Action Line

MISSISSIPPI

Brookhaven Leader
  Generally Speaking

Clarksdale Press Register
  Action Line

Vicksburg Post
  Keeping Posted

MISSOURI

Columbia Missourian
  Show Me

Columbia Tribune
  Action Line

Flat River Journal
  Action Line

Hannibal Courier-Post
  Just Ask Us

Joplin Globe
  Trouble Shooter

Neosho News
  Action Line

Rolla News
  Action Line

Sedalia Capital/Democrat
  Hot Line

NEBRASKA

Fremont Tribune
  Action Desk

Omaha World-Herald
  Action Editor

York News-Times
  Gripe-Pipe

NEW JERSEY

Atlantic City Press
  Mr. Action

Bergen County Record
  Action Line

Camden Courier-Post
  Gotta Gripe

Dover Daily Advance
  Action Line

Passaic-Clifton Herald-News
  Speak Up

Somerville Courier-News
  Help!

Trenton Evening Times
  Action Line

NEW MEXICO

Albuquerque Journal
  Action Line

Las Cruces Sun News
  Sounding Board

NEW YORK

Auburn Citizen Advisor
  That's A Good Question

Brooklyn Today
  Action Line

Buffalo Courier-Press
  Courier Action

Buffalo Evening News
  News Power

Elmira Star Gazette
  Help!

Ithaca Journal
  Help

Mamaroneck Times
  Help!

Mount Vernon Argus
  Help!

Niagara Falls Gazette
  Help!

New York News
  Action Line

Oneonta Star
  Action Line

Portchester Item
  Help!

Rochester Democrat & Chronicle
  Help!

Tarrytown News
  Help!

Troy Times Record
  Hot Line

Utica Observer Dispatch
  Help!

White Plains Reporter Dispatch
  Help!

Yonkers Herald Statesman
  Help!

NORTH CAROLINA

Charlotte Observer/News
  Quest; Tell It Line

Concord Tribune
  Mr. Trib

Charlotte News
  Action Line (Tell-It Line)

Fayetteville Observer
  Live Wire

High Point Enterprise
  Action Line

Lumberton Robesonian
  Action Line

Raleigh Times
  Hotline

Reedsville Review
  Public Eye

Rocky Mount Telegram
  Open Line

Salisbury Post
  Ask Us

Wilson Times
  Whiz Line

NORTH DAKOTA

Devils Lake Journal
  Action Line

OHIO

Akron Beacon Journal
  Action Line

Cincinnati Enquirer
  Action Line

Cleveland Press
  Action Line

Dayton Journal Herald
  Action Line

Defiance Crescent-News
  Action Line

Hamilton Journal-News
  Action Line

Lorain Journal
  Hot Line

Niles Times
  Here's Your Answer

Toledo Blade
  ZIP line

Troy News
  Action Line

Willoughby-Menton News-Herald
  Hot Line

OKLAHOMA

Oklahoma City Times
  Action Line

Tulsa Daily World
  Action Line

Vinita Journal
  Ask 'n Answer

OREGON

Grants Pass Courier
  Action Line (Dispatches)

PENNSYLVANIA

Beaver Falls News-Tribune
  Action Line

Bethlehem Globe-Times
  Action Line

Bradford Era
  Round The Square

Columbia News
  Mirror of Public Opinion

Easton Express
  Action Express

Ellwood City Ledger
  Action Line

Greensburg Tribune Review
  Action Line

Lancaster News
  The Public Eye

Philadelphia Bulletin
  Mr. Fixit

Pottsville Republican
  Action Line

Shamokin News-Item
  Action Line

Sunbury Daily Item
  Action Line

Washington-Observer-Reporter
  Action

RHODE ISLAND

Providence Journal/Bulletin
  Ask Us

SOUTH CAROLINA

Greenville Piedmont
   Action Line

SOUTH DAKOTA

Rapid City Journal
   Action Line

TENNESSEE

Athens Post-Athenian
   Action Line

Greenville Sun
   Searchlight

Jackson Sun
   Action/Sun Line

Kingsport Times News
   Action Line

Maryville Alcoa Daily Times
   Action Line

Oak Ridge Oak Ridger
   Action/Hot Line

TEXAS

Abilene Reporter News
   Action Line

Cleburne Times-Review
   Howdy Folks

Corpus Christi Times
   Action Line

Corsicana Sun
   Action Line

Dallas Times-Herald
   Action Line

Denton Record Chronicle
   Contact 33

Fort Worth Star-Telegram
   Action Line

Greenville Herald-Banner
   In Focus

Houston-Chronicle
   Watchem

Laredo Times
   Duty Watch

Port Arthur News
   Box 7-8-9

San Angelo Standard-Times
   Rumor Column

San Antonio Express
   Action

San Antonio News
   Hotline

San Marcos Record
   Action/Hot Line

Texas City Sun
   Hot Line

UTAH

Salt Lake City Desert News
   Do-It Man

VERMONT

Bennington Banner
   Questions Anonymous

VIRGINIA

Fredericksburg Free Lance-Star
   Action Line

Norfolk Ledger-Star
   Action Line

Pulaski Southwest Times
   Action Dial

Roanoke World-News
   Quickline

Williamsburg Virginia Gazette
    Zip Line

WASHINGTON

Port Angeles News
    Ask Capt. Claiam

Seattle Times
    Troubleshooter

WEST VIRGINIA

Charleston Mail
    Hotline

Welch News
    Ridge Runner

WISCONSIN

Merrill Daily Record
    Speak Up

Milwaukee Journal
    Ask the Journal

Wausau Record-Herald
    Speak Up

WYOMING

Riverton Ranger
    Bob Peck's Column

Chapter 11: SPECIFIC COMMUNITY HELP

In addition to state and federal agencies for consumer protection and private organizations geared to help consumers, many states have consumer help on a local level. Counties, and often cities, have their own agencies set up to protect the consumer, and to give advice about consumer problems. With the exception of New Jersey's CALA Program with its far-reaching representation, there is usually at least one county office for consumer affairs. Having an office for consumer affairs in or near your hometown increases your chances for personal contact and service. This section gives a state-by-state listing of county consumer protection offices (they will forward requests for assistance to a city consumer protection office if one is available nearer your hometown). The next time you have a problem, call or drop a line to the office shown below. Keep in mind, though, that not all states have consumer protection offices on local levels, in which case you should use the agencies and organizations outlined in other sections of this book.

ARIZONA

Deputy
Cochise County Attorney's Office
Bisbee, Arizona 85603
(602) 432-2291

Director
Consumer Protection Division
Pima County Attorney's Office
111 West Congress, 9th Floor
Tucson, Arizona 85701
(602) 792-8668

CALIFORNIA

Deputy District Attorney for Consumer
  Protection
Alameda County Office of District
  Attorney
125 12th Street, Room 207
Oakland, California 94607
(415) 874-5656

Director
Del Norte County Division of Consumer Affairs
2650 Washington Boulevard
Crescent City, California 95531
(707) 464-2716 or 3756

Consumer Coordinator
Fresno County Department of Weights & Measures and Consumer Protection
4535 East Hamilton Avenue
Fresno, California 93702
(209) 488-3027

Chief Attorney
Consumer Fraud Division
District Attorney's Office
1100 Van Ness Avenue
Fresno, California 93721
(209) 488-3050

Deputy District Attorney Consumer Unit
Kern County District Attorney's Office
11415 Truxton Avenue
Bakersfield, California 93301
(805) 861-2443

Director, Los Angeles County
Consumer & Environment Protection Division
District Attorney's Office
540 Hall of Records
320 West Temple
Los Angeles, California 90012
(213) 974-3974

Marin County
Consumer Services Deputy
Human Relations Department
Civic Center, Room 276
San Rafael, California 94903
(415) 479-1100, Ext. 2971

District Attorney
Consumer Fraud Division
Hall of Justice, Civic Center
Room 155
San Rafael, California 94903
(415) 479-1100

Director, Monterey County
Department of Consumer Affairs
1220 Natividad Road
Salinas, California 93901
(408) 758-3859

Deputy District Attorney
Consumer Fraud Unit
District Attorney's Office
P. O. Box 1369
Salinas, California 93901
(408) 758-4626

Napa County, District Attorney
810 Brown Street
Napa, California 94558
(707) 224-7967

Deputy District Attorney in Charge
Major Fraud and Economic Crime Division
District Attorney's Office
P.O. Box 808, 700 Civic Center Dr., W.
Santa Ana, California 92702
(714) 834-3600

Deputy District Attorney
Riverside County Consumer Unit
District Attorney's Office
P. O. Box 1148
Riverside, California 92501
(714) 787-6372

Sacramento County
Supervising District Attorney, Fraud Division
District Attorney's Office
P. O. Box 749
Sacramento, California 95804
(916) 440-6823

Director
Consumer Protection Bureau
816 "H" Street, Room 104
Sacramento, California 95814
(916) 454-2113 or 2417

Director, San Bernardino County
Department of Weights and Measures & Consumer Affairs
160 East 6th Street
San Bernardino, California 92415
(714) 383-1411

Deputy District Attorney in
　Charge, Consumer Fraud
District Attorney's Office
Courthouse, Room 200
San Bernardino, California 92415
(714) 383-1134

Director, San Diego County
Consumer Fraud Division
District Attorney's Office
220 West Broadway
San Diego, California 92101
(714) 236-2382

San Francisco County
Assistant District Attorney
Consumer Fraud Division
District Attorney's Office
880 Bryant Street, Room 301
San Francisco, California 94103
(415) 553-1030

San Luis Obispo County
District Attorney
Consumer Unit
District Attorney's Office
302 Courthouse Annex
San Luis Obispo, California 93401
(805) 543-3464

San Mateo County
Deputy District Attorney
Hall of Justice and Records
Redwood City, California 94063
(415) 364-5600

Santa Barbara County
Deputy in Charge
Consumer Business Law Section
District Attorney's Office
118 East Figueroa Street
Santa Barbara, California 93101
(805) 963-1441

Director, Santa Clara County
Department of Weights and Meas-
　ures & Consumer Affairs
1555 Berger Drive
San Jose, California 95112
(408) 299-2105

Deputy District Attorney
Consumer Fraud Unit
232 East Gish Road
San Jose, California 95112
(408) 275-9651

Director, Santa Cruz County
Department of Weights and Measures
　& Consumer Affairs
640 Capitola Road
Santa Cruz, California 95602
(408) 425-2054

Solano County
Deputy District Attorney
Consumer Fraud Unit
Hall of Justice, 600 Union Avenue
Fairfield, California 94533
(707) 429-6451

Sonoma County
Deputy District Attorney
Consumer Fraud Unit
2555 Mendocino Avenue, P.O. Box 1964
Santa Rosa, California 95403
(707) 527-2641

Stanislaus County
Consumer Affairs Coordinator
Office of Consumer Affairs
725 B County Center #3
Modesto, California 95355
(209) 525-6211

Deputy District Attorney
Consumer Fraud Unit
P. O. Box 442
Modesto, California 95353
(209) 526-6345

Sutter County
Assistant District Attorney
Consumer Unit
Courthouse Annex
Yuba City, California 95991
(916) 673-5058

Director, Ventura County
Department of Weights and
　Measures & Consumer Affairs
608 El Rio Drive
Oxnard, California 93030
(805) 487-7711, Ext. 4377

Consumer Fraud Section
District Attorney's Office
501 Poli Street
Ventura, California 93001
(805) 648-6131, Ext. 2537

COLORADO

Director, Adams, Arapahoe, Boulder,
  Denver & Jefferson Counties
Metropolitan District Attorney's
  Consumer Office
655 South Broadway
Denver, Colorado 80209
(303) 777-3072

Chief Deputy District Attorney
El Paso & Teller Counties (4th Judicial District)
Consumer Affairs Division
District Attorney's Office
303 South Cascade, Suite B
Colorado Springs, Colorado 80902
(303) 473-3801

District Attorney, Archuleta, LaPlata
  & San Juan Counties
P. O. Box 1062
Durango, Colorado 80301
(303) 247-8850

Consumer Affairs Specialist
Pueblo County
District Attorney's Office
County Courthouse, Room 344
Pueblo, Colorado 81003
(303) 543-3550

CONNECTICUT

Office of Consumer Protection
City Hall
Middletown, Connecticut 06457
(203) 347-4671

FLORIDA

Coordinator, Brevard County (18th
  Judicial District)
Consumer Fraud Division
State Attorney's Office
County Courthouse
Titusville, Florida 32780
(305) 269-8421

Director, Broward County
Office of Consumer Affairs
200 S.E. 6th Street, Room 202
Fort Lauderdale, Florida 33301
(305) 765-5307

Director, Dade County
Consumer Protection Division
Metropolitan Dade County
140 West Flagler St., 16th Floor
Miami, Florida 33130
(305) 579-4222

State Attorney, DeSota, Manatee,
  Sarasota Counties (12th Judicial Circuit)
2078 Main Street
Sarasota, Florida 33577
(813) 955-0918

Director, Hillsboro County
Hillsboro County Department of
  Consumer Affairs
205 Marion Street
Tampa, Florida 33602
(813) 272-6750

Director, Palm Beach County
Department of Consumer Affairs
301 North Olive Avenue
West Palm Beach, Florida 33401
(305) 837-2670

Consumer Fraud Division
Office of State Attorney
County Courthouse, Room 430
West Palm Beach, Florida 33401
(305) 659-4222

Director, Pinellas County
Office of Consumer Affairs
315 Haven Street
Clearwater, Florida 33516
(813) 441-8976

GEORGIA

Director
Office of Consumer Affairs
City Hall, Memorial Drive Annex
121 Memorial Drive, S.W.
Atlanta, Georgia 30303
(404) 658-6704

Consumer Affairs Specialist
Community Relations Commission
Memorial Drive Annex
121 Memorial Drive, S.W.
Atlanta, Georgia 30303
(404) 659-4463, Ext. 433

HAWAII

City Information and Complaints Office
Honolulu County, City Hall
Honolulu, Hawaii 96813
(808) 546-7079

IDAHO

Consumer Affairs Office
Idaho State University
Pocatello, Idaho 83201
(208) 236-2803

ILLINOIS

Director, Cook County
Consumer Complaint Division
Office of State's Attorney
Civic Center, Suite 303
Randolph at Clark
Chicago, Illinois 60602
(312) 443-8425

Director, Rock Island County
Consumer Protection Division
Office of State's Attorney
1318 Third Avenue
Rock Island, Illinois 61201
(309) 794-9072

INDIANA

Lake County Prosecuting Attorney
2293 North Main Street
Crown Point, Indiana 46307
(219) 663-1140

Assistant to Prosecutor
Consumer Protection Division
400 Broadway, Room 104
Gary, Indiana 46402
(219) 886-3621, Ext. 385

Department of Public Safety and Consumer Protection
2542 City-County Building
Indianapolis, Indiana 46204
(317) 633-3680

KANSAS

Assistant District Attorney and Head, Johnston County
Consumer Protection Division
District Attorney's Office
County Courthouse, Box 728
Olathe, Kansas 66061
(913) 782-5000, Ext. 318

Director, Sedgewick County
Consumer Protection Division
District Attorney's Office
County Courthouse, 5th Floor
Wichita, Kansas 67203
(316) 268-7405

Assistant District Attorney, Wyandotte County
Consumer Protection Division
District Attorney's Office
710 North 7th Street
Kansas City, Kansas 66102
(913) 371-1600, Ext. 231-234

KENTUCKY

Director, Jefferson County
Consumer Protection Department
208 South 5th Street, Room 401
Louisville, Kentucky 40202

LOUISIANA

Director, East Baton Rouge Parish
Consumer Protection Center
1779 Government Street
Baton Rouge, Louisiana 70802
(504) 344-8506

Director, Jefferson Parish
Consumer Protection and Commercial Frauds Department
District Attorney's Office
1820 Franklin Avenue, Suite 23
Gretna, Louisiana 70053
(504) 366-6611, Ext. 441

MARYLAND

Administrator, Anne Arundel County
Office of Consumer Affairs
Arundel Center, Room 403
Annapolis, Maryland 21404
(301) 268-4300, Ext. 346

Assistant State's Attorney and
  Chief, Baltimore County
Consumer Fraud Division
State Attorney's Office
316 Equitable Building
Baltimore, Maryland 21202
(301) 396-4997

Executive Director, Montgomery
  County
Office of Consumer Affairs
24 Maryland Avenue
Rockville, Maryland 20850
(301) 340-1010

MASSACHUSETTS

Director, Hampshire & Franklin
  Counties
Consumer Protection Agency
District Attorney's Office
Courthouse
Northampton, Massachusetts 01060
(413) 584-1597

Director
Consumer Protection Agency
Courthouse
Greenfield, Massachusetts 01301
(413) 774-5102

MICHIGAN

Assistant Prosecutor, Bay County
Consumer Protection Unit
Office of Prosecuting Attorney
515 Center Avenue
Bay City, Michigan 48706
(517) 893-3594

Assistant Prosecuting Attorney
  and Chief, Genesee County
Consumer Fraud Unit
Office of Prosecuting Attorney
105 Courthouse
Flint, Michigan 48502
(313) 766-8768

Consumer and Business Affairs
  Division, Ingham County
Office of Prosecuting Attorney
101 South Washington
Lansing, Michigan 48933
(517) 482-1517

Assistant Prosecuting Attorney,
  Jackson County
Office of Consumer Protection
506 South Jackson
Jackson, Michigan 49201
(517) 789-7177

Director, Oakland County
Consumer Fraud Division
Oakland County Office of Prosecuting Attorney
1200 North Telegraph
Pontiac, Michigan 48054
(313) 858-0650

Director, Washtenaw County
Consumer Action Center
Consumer Protection Division
Office of Prosecuting Attorney
200 County Building
Main & Huron Streets, Box 645
Ann Arbor, Michigan 48107
(313) 994-2420

Director, Wayne County
Consumer Protection Agency
601 Lafayette Building
144 West Lafayette
Detroit, Michigan 48226
(313) 224-2150

MINNESOTA

Assistant County Attorney and
  Chief, Hennepin County
Citizen Protection Division
County Attorney's Office
County Government Center
Minneapolis, Minnesota 55487
(612) 348-8105

Dakota County Council on Consumer
  Concerns
Dakota County Courthouse
Hastings, Minnesota 55033
(612) 437-4124

MONTANA

Cascade County Attorney
Consumer Protection Division
Great Falls, Montana 59401
(406) 761-6700

Lewis and Clark County Attorney
Consumer Protection Division
Court House
Helena, Montana 59601
(406) 442-4550

NEBRASKA

Douglas County Director
Consumer Fraud Division
County Attorney's Office
Omaha-Douglas Civic Center
18th & Farnam Streets, Room 909
Omaha, Nebraska 68102
(402) 444-7626

NEVADA

Clark County
Chief Deputy District Attorney
District Attorney's Office
Courthouse, 200 East Carson
Las Vegas, Nevada 89101
(702) 386-4011

Washoe County
Investigator in Charge
Consumer Protection Division
District Attorney's Office
P. O. Box 11130
Reno, Nevada 89510
(702) 785-5652

NEW JERSEY

Chairman
Consumer Protection Board
Borough Hall, 309 Main Street
Fort Lee, New Jersey 07024
(201) 947-9400

Chief
Office of Consumer Affairs
355 Main Street
Hackensack, New Jersey 07601
(201) 646-2653

Executive Director
Office of Consumer Affairs
24 Commerce Street, 11th Floor
Newark, New Jersey 07102
(201) 733-3808

Director
Consumer Affairs Division
County Administration Building
640 South Broad Street, Room 116
Trenton, New Jersey 08607
(609) 989-8000

Office of Consumer Affairs
120 Cherry Hill Road
Parsippany, New Jersey 07054
(201) 334-3600 or 335-0700

Chairman
Office of Consumer Affairs
C. N. 2191
Toms River, New Jersey 08753
(201) 244-2121, Ext. 424

Chief
County Administration Building
Somerville, New Jersey 08876
(201) 725-4700, Ext. 306

NEW MEXICO

Director, Bernalillo County
Consumer Protection Division
District Attorney's Office
415 Tijeras, N.W.
Albuquerque, New Mexico 87101
(505) 766-4340

Director, Eddy County
Consumer Affairs Division
District Attorney's Office
P. O. Box 1240
Carlsbad, New Mexico 88220
(505) 885-8822

NEW YORK

Chief, Erie County
Consumer Fraud Bureau
District Attorney's Office
25 Delaware Avenue
Buffalo, New York 14202
(716) 855-2424

Consumer Protection Committee
Office of Erie County Executive
95 Franklin Road
Buffalo, New York 14202
(716) 846-6690

Assistant District Attorney in
  Charge, Kings County
Consumer Frauds & Economic
  Crimes Bureau
District Attorney's Office
210 Joralemon Street
Brooklyn, New York 11201
(212) 643-5100

Consumer Affairs Council
County Office Building, Room 410C
Rochester, New York 14614
(716) 381-1833

Commissioner, Nassau County
Office of Consumer Affairs
160 Old Country Road
Mineola, New York 11501
(516) 535-3282

Assistant District Attorney
Commercial Frauds Bureau
District Attorney's Office
262 Old Country Road
Mineola, New York 11501
(516) 535-3340

Consumer Advocate, Oneida County
County Office Building
800 Park Avenue
Utica, New York 13501
(315) 798-5076

Director, Onondaga County
Office of Consumer Affairs
County Civic Center
421 Montgomery Street
Syracuse, New York 13202
(315) 477-7911

Executive Assistant for Citizen
  Affairs, Rensselaer County
Rensselaer County Courthouse
Troy, New York 12180
(518) 270-5360

Office of Consumer Protection
County Office Building
New Hempstead Road
New City, New York 10956
(914) 638-0500, Ext. 8951

Commissioner, Suffolk County
Department of Consumer Affairs
Suffolk County Center
Veterans Highway
Hauppauge, New York 11787
(516) 979-3100

Chief - Frauds Bureau
District Attorney's Office
Westchester County Courthouse
111 Grove Street
White Plains, New York 10601
(914) 682-2160

Department of Weights & Measures
  and Consumer Affairs
County Office Building
White Plains, New York 10601
(914) 682-3300

NORTH CAROLINA

Fraud Unit, Central Investigations
  Bureau
Charlotte Police Department
Law Enforcement Center
825 East Fourth Street
Charlotte, North Carolina 28205
(704) 374-2311

OHIO

Consumer Fraud Division
Office of Prosecuting Attorney
Hall of Justice, South High Street
Columbus, Ohio 43210
(614) 462-3248

Consumer Protection & Education
  Office
101 East Church Street
Xenia, Ohio 45385
(513) 372-4461

Assistant Prosecuting Attorney,
   Fraud Section
Office of Prosecuting Attorney
County Courts Building
41 North Perry Street, Suite 308
Dayton, Ohio 45402
(513) 228-5126

OKLAHOMA

District Attorney for LeFlore County
County Courthouse
Poteau, Oklahoma 74953
(918) 647-2410, Ext. 2411

PENNSYLVANIA

Director, Allegheny County
Bureau of Consumer Affairs
Jones Law Building, 3rd Floor
4th & Ross Streets
Pittsburgh, Pennsylvania 15219
(412) 355-5402

Department of Transportation, Environmental & Consumer Affairs
News Building, 8th Floor
Scranton, Pennsylvania 18503
(717) 342-8366

County District Attorney
Consumer Protection Commission
County Courthouse
Lancaster, Pennsylvania 17602
(717) 299-4222

TEXAS

Assistant Criminal District Attorney and Chief
Consumer Fraud Division
Office of Criminal District Attorney
San Antonio, Texas 78205
(512) 220-2323

Director, El Paso, Culberson and
   Hudspeth Counties
Consumer Fraud Division
Office of District Attorney
City-County Building, Room 401
El Paso, Texas 79901
(915) 543-2860

Assistant District Attorney
Consumer Fraud Division
Office of District Attorney
301 San Jacinto
Houston, Texas 77002
(713) 228-8311, Ext. 7493

Assistant District Attorney
Consumer Fraud Division
Office of District Attorney
New Criminal Courts Building
300 West Belknap Street
Fort Worth, Texas 76102
(817) 334-1603

Coordinator
Consumer Center of Tarrant County
201 East Belknap Street
Fort Worth, Texas 76102
(817) 334-1784

Consumer Coordinator
Consumer & Housing Office
307 West 7th Street
Austin, Texas 78701
(512) 474-6554

VERMONT

County State's Attorney
439 Main Street
Bennington, Vermont 05201
(802) 442-8116

County State's Attorney
39 Pearl Street, Box 27
Burlington, Vermont 05401
(802) 863-2865

County State's Attorney
County Courthouse
Newport, Vermont 05855
(802) 334-2037

County State's Attorney
34 Main Street
Montpelier, Vermont 05602
(802) 223-2536

County State's Attorney
Middlebury, Vermont 05753
(802) 453-2361

VIRGINIA

Executive Director
Office of Consumer Affairs
2049 15th Street, North
Arlington, Virginia 22201
(703) 558-2142

Director
Department of Consumer Affairs
Erlich Building, Suite 402
4031 University Drive
Fairfax, Virginia 22030
(703) 691-3214

WASHINGTON

Chief Deputy Prosecuting Attorney,
  Fraud Division
County Prosecutor's Office
C517 King County Courthouse
516 Third Avenue
Seattle, Washington 98104
(206) 344-7350

WEST VIRGINIA

Director
Consumer Protection Department
P. O. Box 2749
Charleston, West Virginia 25330
(304) 348-8172

WISCONSIN

District Attorney's Office
County Courthouse
Kenosha, Wisconsin 53140
(414) 657-5135

District Attorney's Office
Wausau, Wisconsin 55401
(715) 842-2141, Ext. 242

Consumer Fraud Division
District Attorney's Office
Safety Building, Room 406E
821 West State Street
Milwaukee, Wisconsin 53233
(414) 278-4792

Director, Consumer Fraud Unit
District Attorney's Office
Stevens Point, Wisconsin 54481
(715) 346-3393

Consumer Fraud Division
District Attorney's Office
730 Wisconsin Avenue
Racine, Wisconsin 53403
(414) 636-3125

Chapter 12: SPECIFIC PROBLEMS

Consumer complaints come in all shapes and sizes. Whatever can be sold, traded, or promised can also break, disappear, or fail to arrive at all. But a surprisingly large number of consumer complaints are concerned with just a few products or industries. This chapter is devoted to those most common problems -- the ones that seem to crop up again and again in surveys across the country. Chances are very good that you will encounter at least some of these problems yourself at some time in your consuming career. It would not be surprising if you or somebody you know encountered all of them. While the general techniques of effective griping apply here as much as to the more unique complaint situation, difficulties in these areas are so common that they deserve some individual attention.

<u>Automobile Repair</u>: This is the granddaddy. We are a nation almost totally dependent on cars for our way of life. In most areas, you simply can't live a normal life unless you can regularly drive or at least be driven where you need to go. Naturally, we are all very anxious whenever the car is out of commission. We want it fixed, fixed right, and fixed now. More consumer complaints, just as naturally, are about getting the car fixed than about any other single thing.

First, there are problems with brand new cars. There is nothing more frustrating than paying thousands of dollars for a factory-fresh automobile that doesn't run right. What's more, the consumer often has to go through incredible pain to get the dealer to fix the same car that only yesterday he had sold as a perfect piece of machinery. The reason, of course, is that the dealer already has what he wants from you, and he can't get any more. Your new car is under warranty, and the dealer will have to be reimbursed by the manufacturer for any repairs he makes while that warranty is still in effect. But the manufacturer is far away -- in Detroit, in Europe, in Japan -- and can't see whether or not a dealer makes repairs. Some dealers are tempted to put your new car back on the lot for a few days, after which they call and say the ping is gone. But it isn't. You and the dealer can play this game for quite some time with no improvement in the situation. You can never prove he isn't trying his best to locate the trouble, and he doesn't have to spend any time on you that he could more profitably spend elsewhere. Once you've driven the new car off the lot, you have lost quite a bit of your power over Smiling Jack, but there are still some things you can do.

1. Refuse to pay. If you're lucky enough to discover a defect before your check clears, stop payment. This will snap old Jack to attention like nothing else. If you're paying on time, stop paying, but make sure there is abundant evidence that you are not in default, only holding out for what is rightfully yours. Return the car to the dealer and refuse to accept it back again until it works. This is plenty hard to do, since you probably bought the car because you need a car, but do it all the same. Try to get the dealer to loan or rent you a car while yours is being fixed. Borrow a car, if you have to, but don't allow the deal to be completed until the car is satisfactory to you.

2. Escalate quickly. As previously mentioned, there isn't much incentive for a dealer to fix your warrantied car once he has banked the purchase price. He will be perfectly happy to have it in the shop until doomsday while you pedal over the icy streets on your two-speed. In this situation, therefore, threats are in order. If you don't get your repairs promptly, go to the top. Take your complaints (and all documentation thereof) to the president of the dealership -- not the manager, but whoever is the top man. Next step: the president of the manufacturing company. Your letter, of course, will follow the form outlined in this book -- demand, history, repeat of demand, plus threat. Depending on the circumstances, you might threaten to have the repairs made elsewhere and bill the company, to return the car and sue for the purchase price, or to launch a campaign against the company's cars. All these tactics are very much more effective if you've bought an American-made car, which is something to keep in mind when making your choice. If you're having problems with a new foreign car or one still under warranty, write to the head of that company in the United States. If you still get no satisfaction, possible remedies are in Small Claims Court, consumer complaint groups such as the National Automobile Dealers Association (see Trade Associations), state and federal consumer protection agencies, and, finally, your lawyer. Also, check your library or bookstore for _What to Do with Your Bad Car: An Action Manual for Lemon Owners_, by Ralph Nader, Lowell Dodge, and Ralf Hotchkiss.

If the warranty has expired on your car, or if the problem is body damage rather than mechanical failure, you have a different set of factors. In the case of functional repairs not covered by warranty, the difficulty is in finding a good, honest mechanic who won't rip you off. In case of body work, you may also have to cope with the insurance company. To find a good repair shop, it helps to know a lot about the work to be done. The more thoroughly you understand cars, the less likely a mechanic is to give you the run-around. But if you don't happen to be an engine buff, there are some things you can do to find good work at a reasonable price. 1. Get an estimate in writing before you have the work done. It's not an iron-clad contract, but it helps. 2. Consult sources. Anybody you know, any organization, such as the Better Business Bureau, that might tell you who does good work. The recommendation of friends and neighbors carries a lot of weight. 3. Let the repairman know that a good job will bring gratitude and repeat business from you, but a rip-off will send you running to complain.

When you're faced with a crumpled fender, you're also faced with a decision: should you involve your insurance company, or not? If the damage is not your fault, then you will certainly want to get the insurance company to pay. If it is, you might want to foot the bill yourself, rather than see your insurance premiums go up. If the burden is on you, you'll probably shop around for the best job, just as in the case of mechanical repairs. If the insurance company pays, you'll have to come to an agreement with the company about reasonable cost. Usually, repair shops that cooperate with insurance adjusters simply don't do the best work. Perhaps they are tempted to process too many claims too fast. But the insurance company will surely call other estimates you get too high. Patient negotiations will usually yield an acceptable compromise. If not, your letters should go to the president of the insurance company, the state insurance department, and the local consumer protection agency. As for unacceptable work on the part of the repair shop, you have the leverage of withheld payment, plus complaints to various agencies, especially any trade associations and the Better Business Bureau.

Banks: Most people never even think of having a dispute with a bank. Organizations, of course, argue with their bankers all the time, but we ordinary folks tend to think the bank must be right, or at least that there's nothing we can do if the bank is wrong. If the problem seems to be a clerical or computer error, and you can't resolve it to your satisfaction in discussions with personnel at the bank, you must determine just what kind of a bank yours is, and complain to the appropriate agency. First, it may be a nationally or state chartered commercial bank. These are the banks which have traditionally offered such services as checking accounts and broad commercial and business loans. These are usually called banks or trusts. If it's a "National" bank or trust, your complaints can be addressed to the Comptroller of the Currency, United States Department of the Treasury, Washington, D. C. 20220. In the case of commercial banks chartered by the states, you can complain either to the nearest Federal Reserve Bank, or to the Federal Deposit Insurance Corporation (FDIC) if the bank is so insured. Once in a while, one runs across a bank that is not a member of any federal organization. In the first place, it's better not to bank with such an organization. But if you already have, you can complain to the department of banking practices in your state.

In making complaints about a savings and loan institution

(that's the kind that traditionally gives slightly higher interest on your savings but doesn't offer checking, though these distinctions are changing), write to the Federal Home Loan Bank Board, 101 Indiana Avenue, N.W., Washington, D. C. 20552, or to the Federal Savings and Loan Insurance Corporation, same address.

The only other common institution that performs banking functions is the Credit Union. These usually offer minimal services at low rates to members. If you belong to such an organization -- usually through your club or your job -- you can write to the National Credit Union Administration, Office of Examination and Insurance, 2025 M Street, N.W., Washington, D. C. 20456. If your Credit Union is not federally chartered, you will have to turn again to the state department of banking. (For a discussion of problems with loans and credit, see Credit, this chapter.)

Credit, Billing, and Debt Collection: Many of the worst abuses perpetrated on consumers by billers -- especially credit card companies -- have been eliminated or reduced by the Fair Credit Billing Act of 1976 and other recent laws affecting disclosure and information. It is illegal for anyone to send you a bill whose due date is the next day, for instance, or to fail to respond to a customer's disputing of charges made. The federal laws apply to credit card companies, but you will find that most large billing entities, such as the Telephone Company or department stores, also abide by these rules, in some cases in compliance with state laws. You may want to dispute a bill because you are being billed for goods or services you have found to be unsatisfactory. If you think the creditor has made an error in calculating what you owe, the best strategy is the typical ladder of escalating complaints, beginning with the highest-placed company official you can reach on the phone. Make your complaint immediately upon reception of the bill, well before the amount is due, if possible. You will be treated with more courtesy and sympathy if you bring up the matter before you are in arrears. If you have the proper documentation, and if you manage to reach somebody both rational and responsible, such matters are usually resolved. Just remember, don't pay until you are satisfied with the solution. It's much harder to get money back than to withhold it in the first place.

If the problem is not a technical error but poor treatment of one kind or another, you are not obligated to pay unless you can be proved wrong. This means that the creditor will have to take you to court, in the extreme case, to recover his money. If you feel confident that you could demonstrate you had not been properly served, simply say so, and don't pay. Of course, if the bill is for more than one item, you should pay for all but the disputed goods or services. This strategy is equally good if the billing organization is not the company from which you bought the disputed item. If you have charged something on your credit card, for example, which has subsequently proved unsatisfactory, don't pay. Notify the credit card company that you did, indeed, charge an inflatable swimsuit from Dunkee's, Inc., but that the garment failed to inflate on every trial, and that you have sent it back with a notice that you do not accept it. The card company can either sue you to recover the debt, or return the debt to the store for collection. In almost all cases, they will do the latter. From then on, your dispute is with the party of the first part. The same goes for a collection agency. If you have a good reason not to pay the original creditor, you have just as good a reason not to pay a third party to whom collection has been assigned. Tell the collection company just what you told the store: the swimsuit doesn't inflate, and you don't pay.

What if your credit problem involves a difficulty with getting a credit card or a loan? In any such case, you have a right to know why you are being turned down. If, for example, you have an unfavorable file with a credit bureau that causes you to be refused for loans or charge accounts, you have a right to know what the problem is, and a right to look at the file. That way, if false or misleading information about your suitability as a credit risk is being sent around, you can contest it. Under the Fair Credit Reporting Act, a credit bureau to which you complain must investigate what is in your file. If, after such an investigation, the credit bureau still thinks you deserve its bad report, it must also include in its file (which it supplies to employers, loan companies, banks, and the like for a fee) a report <u>written by you</u> stating what you think is wrong with the bureau's estimate of your credit worthiness. It may be harder to find out if, for example, an insurance company is circulating the word among other insurance companies that you are a bad risk, but it can be done. Get in touch with your local office of the Federal Trade Commission or the appropriate regulatory agency.

<u>Delivery</u>: This isn't a section about obstetrics, though there can be consumer problems even attending a Blessed Event (see Medical Services, this chapter). Instead, this is the kind of delivery that you <u>don't</u> get, after staying home from work all day or going without a stove for three weeks in anticipation of the bronze beauty that was

supposed to arrive on the fifteenth. A truly amazing number of consumer complaints involve missed delivery dates, deliveries to the wrong address, deliveries of the wrong merchandise, and so forth. If you always charge items to be delivered later, you always have the option of simply cancelling out on an order that fails to show up at the appointed hour. Admittedly, there are times when it's very hard to do. If you really want the merchandise anyway, start your round of complaints. Remember, reach as high as you can, and demand, report, demand, threaten. If you have already paid actual cash, insist on your money back. Once you have decided to request a refund, don't accept the merchandise, not if they send it out in the middle of the night. Tell the store that a dress for your cousin's wedding is of no use to you three weeks after the ceremony. In the case of delivery of the wrong merchandise, it again depends on how much you want to fight. If the item delivered is pretty much like what you wanted, and large, it might be just as well to relax and enjoy. But if you determine that the item is unacceptable, make them take it back. A man in Minnesota got prompt removal of a "hideous" green refrigerator by threatening -- quite convincingly -- to hire a truck and have the offending appliance deposited in the store's executive office suite if it wasn't retrieved within the week.

<u>Door-to-Door Sales</u>: The typical door-to-door salesperson is the encyclopedia pusher with the slicked-back hair, expensive suit, and a mile-a-minute sales pitch. There's a grain of truth in the stereotype, too, especially when it comes to encyclopedias. Salesmen have been known to pose as employees of the local school, delivering a fast-paced line designed to convince parents that they aren't doing right by their children if they don't buy a whole set. Then there are

the phoney "discounts" if a family agrees to pose for advertisements, and the "free" volumes that aren't free at all. Many customers find themselves hornswoggled into purchasing something they had no need or desire for ten minutes before the salesman appeared, nor do they want it ten minutes after he's gone. Fortunately, many states have a three-day "cooling-off" rule that allows you to back out of any deal made with a salesman if you send a letter of cancellation within three days. The Federal Trade Commission (see "Federal Agencies") has such a regulation, too, for purchases of over $25. Under this rule, the salesman has to give you a "notice of cancellation" at the time of the purchase. If the seller doesn't return your money, he may be liable to a fine of up to $10,000. Your knowledge of this fact, if you mention it in your letter, will probably insure that you'll have no more trouble. The FTC regulation doesn't apply, however, if your purchase was insurance, securities, real estate, or work supplies.

Funeral Parlors: Consumers are becoming increasingly aware that some of the most deceptive business practices in our society today are perpetrated on us just at the time -- the moments after the death of a loved one -- when we are least able to defend ourselves. Because we don't like to think about death, we are often unprepared and disoriented when it happens. Funeral directors and others in the business take advantage of this vulnerable time to sell us thousands of dollars worth of embalming, caskets, funeral ceremonies, flowers, and burial vaults. If we murmer a word of protest, we are skillfully made to feel like revolting skinflints to think about cost "at a time like this." When the whole thing is over, we realize that two or three or five thousand dollars have been invested in the dead person's funeral.

Often, the dead person would much rather have seen such funds invested in the living. If ever an industry was ripe for a consumer revolution, it is the funeral business.

One way to avoid being taken advantage of at the moment of death is to discuss with those close to you what each one wishes for his or her funeral. This need not be morbid, for death, as everyone knows, is a fact of life.

You should know that in spite of what a funeral home employee may tell you, in most cases, public health laws do not require embalming, fancy caskets, or vaults. If you choose cremation, only two states, Massachusetts and Michigan, require that the body be cremated in a casket. You can ask for, and should get, a simple cardboard box for cremation. In addition, you should be aware that funeral directors often don't show the low-priced caskets. You have to ask (and get dirty looks and disparaging remarks about your insensitivity), after which you are reluctantly led to a bare back room where the "cheap" -- only a few hundred dollars -- caskets are kept.

To avoid being involved in a mounting spiral of pressure and a costly, wasteful funeral, do not call a funeral home until you are certain of what you want. Once a body has been removed from the place of death, it is almost impossible to get the funeral director to release it again. There are alternatives to the traditional high-priced American funeral. The best time to find out about them is before you need to know. Write to the Continental Association of Funeral and Memorial Societies, Suite 1100, 1828 L Street, N.W., Washington, D. C. 20036. If death overtakes someone in your family suddenly, try to get in touch with your local memorial society, if there is one, and ask if you can become an instant member, or if they can advise you. Memorial societies are groups of consumers banded together to beat the high cost of death and the inhumane high-pressure tactics of the funeral industry.

<u>Health Clubs</u>: The modern interest in physical fitness has made the health club or spa the inheritor of all the deceptive practices that used to be the province of dancing lesson studios. In each case, you are required to sign up for a series of lessons or sessions, and to pay in advance. It subsequently proves to be impossible to pry any refund out of the club, no matter how compelling your excuse for not finishing the course. In an even worse dodge, a club will take memberships even before it opens -- and then never open. The best way to avoid being had is to shop around for a club that will take a small advance deposit, or join one that provides free access to facilities for a flat fee. Try to avoid long pay-in-advance contracts for dancing lessons, too, just in case you've been struck by disco fever. Address complaints to your nearest consumer protection agency.

<u>Home Improvement</u>: This is an area ripe for swindlers, and thus for complaints. We're not talking about having good old Mel, who's lived down the block for ten years, build that addition at long last. Complaints don't arise from deals with well-known, reputable contractors, but from cheap jobs, often sold door-to-door, done (or not done) by strangers who then leave town with your money. The "improvements" offered can range from a new roof to painting, extermination, new siding, new swimming pools, even body work on the family car.

Sometimes, these fly-by-night workmen take your money, move a few dollars worth of supplies onto your property, and disappear. When you finally realize that they aren't coming back, they're long gone. But if you think that's the worst that can happen, you're wrong. You may be in a worse fix if they actually begin or even finish the job. That way, you won't find out until your basement starts leaking in the fall that you've been had. To add insult to injury, such so-called contractors sometimes try to sue you to get you to pay for contracted work, even if the work is no good. Clearly, you should never hire anybody whose reputation is unknown to do any repairs around the house. If you do take a chance, don't fork over any money until after the job is done. Don't worry about signing a contract, however. According to provisions of the Truth in Lending Act of 1968, you cannot be forced to pay for contracted work if you can demonstrate that quality implied in the contract has not been provided. Since this act was passed by Congress, few itinerant improvers have actually brought a case into court. For the most part, such disputes are now settled before trial, in favor of the consumer. For complaints about work done at your home, call your consumer protection agency.

<u>Landlords (and Tenants)</u>: If you've ever read a standard lease -- the printed kind with pages and pages of itty-bitty print -- you know that all the chips are in the landlord's corner. It is the landlord who can decide to terminate your lease on a moment's notice, a landlord who can enter the premises without warning, who can evict you for playing your clarinet or shaking your rug out the window, or just because he feels like it. Until very recently, the only right a tenant had was to hunker down, hope for the best, and pay the rent on time.

But lately, many of these standard leases are being successfully challenged in court. Courts in several states have recognized that the landlord, in taking on a tenant in the first place, implicitly agrees to provide habitable quarters. If the tenant isn't getting what he paid for, in other words, he no longer has to pay. This means that if you feel conditions in your apartment or house are untenable, and repeated requests to the landlord have brought no action, you are justified in withholding rent. Furthermore, you must not be subject to retaliatory eviction because you joined a tenant's group or participated in a rent strike.

Few tenants, no matter how difficult their living conditions have become, want to hold out the rent without any group support. Nor should you do so, even if you want to. The limits on what's allowed vary from state to state, and you might be breaking the law without knowing exactly what it is. In some states, the tenant is allowed to make needed repairs and then deduct the cost from the rent, up to a certain maximum. In other states, this is not allowed, and you may get stuck for the cost yourself. Besides habitability, the chief tenant problem is getting back the security deposit. Tenant's groups can help you with that, too, since most states put a limit on the amount of security deposits. If you don't know how to get in touch with a tenant's rights group in your area, try asking the local housing authority, or the regional office of the Department of Housing and Development (HUD). Another source of this kind of information is the Legal Aid Office, or any other legal group involved in public interest law.

<u>Lawyers</u>: Most of us go through life without legal advice, except maybe to make a will. Partly, we just don't know how to go about getting

a lawyer we can trust, and partly we aren't aware of the benefits of having competent legal help on one's side. There are many consumer problems which could be handled more effectively for you by somebody well versed in consumer issues. If you don't have any idea how to go about getting a lawyer, call the local Legal Aid organization or Bar Association. Even if your income is too high to qualify for Legal Aid, they can point you in the right direction. Lawyers, as everybody knows, charge a lot for their services. But you might be able to arrange for reduced fees if you find an attorney sympathetic to your case. If you need advice on a specific point of law, try writing the National Consumer Law Center in Boston, Massachusetts. Or, when you call the Bar Association for information, say you'd like the names of two or three lawyers specifically interested in this kind of public-interest case.

Medical Services: Until recently, most patients thought themselves too ignorant to complain about the treatment they received from a doctor or dentist. Unless serious disability had resulted, nobody thought of filing a malpractice suit. But the consumer movement, the women's movement, and others have brought to the public's attention that doctors are human, and fallible, just like the rest of us. If you feel you are being treated badly by an individual practitioner, the best thing to do is tell him so. Many old-fashioned medical people are astonished to learn, for example, that patients need and want to know the exact nature of their illnesses, even if they are terminal. If doctors are informed of the patient's real desires, they are usually willing to comply with reasonable requests. On the other hand, if you think your practitioner habitually engages in shoddy or hurtful practices, report him to the county medical society.

In disputes with hospitals or nursing homes, try to find out if the institution has a person hired to handle complaints. Hospital patient advocates are usually pretty sympathetic and surprisingly effective, where they exist at all. Otherwise, as usual, shoot for the top. Address your complaint letter to the chairman of the hospital board or the owner of the nursing home. Both these types of care facilities have had a run of bad publicity in recent times, and they are eager to stay clear of any more. Suggest in your letter that if your complaints are not attended to, you will send copies of your next letter to the state health department, the local consumer protection agency, and perhaps the city council.

Travel: Most people travel these days by car, by bus, or by air. If you have a problem concerning trains, it's hard to get any satisfaction, because of the desparate state of the National Railroad Passenger Corp. (AMTRAK). You should, if you want to complain, direct your letters to the national headquarters of AMTRAK, 955 L'Enfant Plaza North, S.W., Washington, D. C. 20260. And tell them, while you're at it, that we would all like to see the return of real rail passenger service in the United States.

A car problem is a car problem, and discussed elsewhere. That leaves busses and planes. The national offices of Greyhound Lines, Inc. are located in the Greyhound Tower, Phoenix, Arizona 85013. National Trailways Bus System is at 1200 I Street, N.W., Washington, D. C. 20005. If letters to these addresses don't get you what you want, you can also direct complaints to the Interstate Commerce Commission, Washington, D. C. 20423.

In airline travel, most foul-ups occur on the run, making effective complaining even more difficult. If you arrive to find your flight cancelled or full, even though you've had a reservation for weeks, don't despair. Recent regulations provide refunds, accommodations, even free flights for passengers so treated. Try to speak to a supervisor at once, letting him or her know that you know about such rules. Be clear about what you want, and you'll probably get it. If you just want your family to arrive comfortably in Chicago within the next twenty-four hours, the airline will be able to fill that request and make you comfortable in the meantime, too. If, on the other hand, it is vital to your business that you arrive in Duluth no later than two hours from your scheduled arrival, tell the airline that. They may be able to arrange for you to make it, even if you don't exactly ride like a prince.

If the problem is with your luggage rather than with your flight, try hard to keep cool. Most lost luggage does show up, usually straggling along on a later flight because of missed connections or other handling problems. If your bags are actually lost, you are entitled to up to $500 compensation, but that's all. Don't take valuables above that amount in your luggage, and make sure that if you carry them on the plane with you, you also carry them off. Cameras, musical instruments, and the like have a way of vanishing very soon after you deplane, and if you haven't entrusted them to the airline's care in the first place, they have no obligation to them.

The other common complaint of travelers is about travel agencies. In part, this is a situation of careful consuming. You can have a travel agent arrange for your airline tickets absolutely free, and it certainly can save time and headaches. But how can you know if the agent has gotten you the lowest possible fare, unless you know what the fare is? If you later find out you could have done much better for yourself, perhaps next time you should do it yourself. If, on the other hand, an agency arranges a vacation in Mexico that's worse than two weeks in the county jail, you have a more legitimate basis for complaint. You can't be expected to know what is a good hotel in Mexico City. Complain first, of course, to the head of the travel agency that booked you into the fleabag. If that gets you nowhere, write to the American Society of Travel Agents, 360 Lexington Avenue, New York, New York 10017, with copies to your local consumer protection agency.

Unfair and Deceptive Trade Practices: These are essentially cons; tricks pulled on you by businesses or individuals that are illegal, but that you might not know to be illegal. First off, there's fraud. Fraud isn't just a matter of a seller not giving you what you were promised. He has to know he doesn't intend to make good on the promise, even as he makes it. If you have hard, physical evidence that you've been defrauded, report it at once to the state Attorney General's office, and to the state consumer protection agency.

Deceptive advertising is a thorn in the side of the consuming public, and should be reported to whatever agencies you can think of, starting with the National Advertising Review Board (see Trade Associations). As for getting what you want from the advertiser, it is often very effective to simply ask the head of the company how he thinks his ad would be viewed by the consumer protection agency or the Attorney General. Some variants of deceptive advertising are illegal as such, particularly what is known as the "bait and switch" technique.

In the scenario for this one, a store advertises an item at an attractive price, but when you get to the store, none of the advertised items are available. Instead, you are encouraged to buy a similar but more costly model. If this happens to you, tell the salesman or the head of the store that you want the advertised merchandise at the advertised price, or you will be consulting with legal authorities.

Pyramid schemes, which are variants of the chain letter gimmick, are also illegal in most areas. (This doesn't mean the kind of chain letter that urges you to send a recipe for spaghetti sauce to five other people, but the kind that urges you to send money.) The reason these schemes are illegal is that they don't work. Even with recipes. It's just that if you send out five recipes and get only one back, not too much has been lost. But if you send out five hundred dollars in the hope of receiving much more from "sub-distributors" further down the line, you've been had. Only those who are in on the scheme at the beginning can make large profits. If you are approached by someone who offers to make you rich by allowing you to buy and then sell a distributorship for some product, report him to your state Attorney General. Never give such people any money, but report them anyway. If they are engaged in pyramiding, you could save some of your fellow consumers from ruin. One way to tell a pyramid scheme from a legitimate franchise or distributorship is that the business that's on the up-and-up will emphasize its product, not how you can clean up by drawing others into the scheme.

Another ploy, illegal in some states but not in all, is referral or showcase selling. This is a favorite of door-to-door salesmen, who will quote you a price -- usually grossly inflated -- but quickly say that you can get discounts for referring others to them or for using your item as a model to encourage sales to the neighbors. If you hear such an offer, focus your attention on the price quoted. This is what the salesperson doesn't want you to do. You're supposed to be thinking about the big chunks each referral will take off the price. If the original quote seems reasonable to you, it's probably not a tricky deal. Usually, though, when you eliminate the hoopla, you'll see that you're being magnificently overcharged. If you've already fallen for such a line, discovering later that you can't interest a single friend in your "showcase" merchandise, you may have some chance to get some of your money back. Call the local consumer protection agency and ask if such tactics are legal, and if not, what remedies are open to you.

NOTES

NOTES

NOTES

NOTES

NOTES